Tasteful Entertaining

A collection of recipes for family, friends and get-togethers

This book is published by Lifevest Publishing Inc., Centennial, Colorado. No portion of this book may be reproduced without the expressed written consent of Lifevest Publishing and Barry Keefe.

Tasteful Entertaining is written by Chef Barry Keefe
Copyright 2005, Barry Keefe

Published and Printed by:
  Lifevest Publishing
  4901 E. Dry Creek Rd., #170
  Centennial, CO 80122
  www.lifevestpublishing.com

Printed in the United States of America

I.S.B.N. 1-59879-084-6

Tasteful Entertaining

A collection of recipes for family, friends and get-togethers

By Chef Barry Keefe

Thank you

I would like to thank my wife Rachael, son Logan and Mom Irene. Without your support this never would have been possible.

Thank you
and I love you all.

Table of Contents

Soups
1-8
****

Salsas
9-17
****

Salads
18-41
****

Starters
42-68
****

Side Dishes
69-92
****

Sandwiches, Burgers Pizzas & Calzones
93-107
****

Seafood
108-119
****

Poultry
120-133
****

Beef, Pork & Lamb
134-145
******

Sunday Brunch
146-158
******

Sweet Endings
159-174
******

Index
175-179
******

Soups

BRUSCHETTA SOUP
(with cheesy bread croutons)

Serving size- 1 large soup crock

Ingredients:
3 tablespoons extra virgin olive oil
3 cups finely diced plum tomatoes
1 large finely diced red onion
1 tablespoon fresh chopped garlic
1/4 cup balsamic vinegar
3 cups vegetable broth
2 cups tomato juice
2 tablespoons finely chopped fresh basil leaves
1 teaspoon pepper
1 teaspoon salt
1/4 cup butter
1/2 loaf crusty Italian bread (diced)
1/2 cup grated romano cheese

Method:
1. Drizzle olive oil in a large stockpot over medium heat.
2. Sauté tomatoes, onion and garlic for about 5 minutes stirring occasionally.
3. To the stock pot, add vinegar, broth, tomato juice, basil, pepper and salt. Bring pot to a boil then lower heat to a simmer and cook for 30 minutes.
4. Melt butter in a large skillet over medium high heat. Add bread croutons and continue stirring until crispy and golden brown. Toss with romano cheese.
5. Serve soup in a large crock and top with croutons.

FIRE PIT CHILI

Serving size- 1 large soup crock

Ingredients:
3 tablespoons extra virgin olive oil
2 lbs ground beef (85% lean)
1 lb ground pork
1 large finely diced red onion
1 large finely diced red bell pepper
1 large finely diced green bell pepper
2 cups canned dark red kidney beans (drained)
3 cups canned crushed tomatoes
1/4 cup dark chili powder
2 tablespoons dried cumin
1 tablespoon dried oregano
1 teaspoon pepper
1 teaspoon salt
(garnish) shredded Monterey jack cheese
(garnish) sour cream

Method:
1. Drizzle olive oil in a large stockpot over medium heat.
2. Sauté ground beef, pork, onions and both peppers for about 10-15 minutes stirring occasionally.
3. Add beans, crushed tomatoes, chili powder, cumin, oregano, pepper and salt. Simmer on low heat for about 1 hour.
4. Serve in a large crock and top with shredded cheese and sour cream.

CHILLED STRAWBERRY CHAMPAGNE SOUP

Serving size- 1 large soup crock

Ingredients:
4 quarts fresh strawberries (washed and stems removed)
1/2 gallon water
1 cup champagne
1 cup sugar
1/4 cup honey
1 tablespoon finely chopped fresh mint leaves

Method:
1. Place strawberries in a large stockpot with water, champagne and sugar. Bring to a boil. Remove from heat.
2. Drain strawberries from liquid and puree in a food processor. Add strawberry purée back to liquid with honey and mint.
3. Refrigerate soup for 24 hours.
4. Serve in a large soup crock.

TORTELLINI SOUP

Serving size- 1 large soup crock

Ingredients:
2 tablespoons extra virgin olive oil
1 teaspoon chopped fresh garlic
1 small finely diced red onion
2 cups finely diced plum tomatoes
8 oz bag baby spinach leaves (chopped)
6 cups chicken broth
2 small bags frozen cheese tortellini
1 teaspoon finely chopped fresh basil leaves
1/2 teaspoon pepper
1/2 teaspoon salt
(garnish) grated romano cheese

Method:
1. Drizzle extra virgin olive oil in a large stockpot over medium heat.
2. Sauté garlic, onions, tomatoes and spinach for about 5 minutes stirring occasionally.
3. Add chicken broth, tortellini, basil, pepper and salt. Bring to a boil, then lower heat to a simmer for 10 minutes.
4. Serve in a large soup crock and garnish with romano cheese.

CREAMY TOMATO GORGONZOLA BISQUE

Serving size- 1 large soup crock

Ingredients:
2 tablespoons extra virgin olive oil
1 small finely diced white onion
3 cups canned crushed tomatoes
2 cups vegetable broth
1 cup heavy cream
8 oz crumbled gorgonzola cheese
1 tablespoon finely chopped fresh basil leaves
1 teaspoon onion powder
1 teaspoon garlic powder
1 teaspoon pepper
1 teaspoon salt

Method:
1. Drizzle extra virgin olive oil in a large stockpot over medium heat.
2. Sauté onions and tomatoes for about 5 minutes stirring occasionally.
3. Add vegetable broth and bring to a boil.
4. Add all other ingredients and lower heat to a simmer. Cook soup for about 35 minutes, stirring frequently.
5. Serve in a large soup crock.

 # GASPACHO

Serving size- 1 large soup crock

Ingredients:
1 large finely diced red onion
1 large finely diced red bell pepper
1 large finely diced green bell pepper
1 large finely diced seedless cucumber (peeled)
2 cups finely diced plum tomatoes
1 quart tomato juice
1/4 cup lime juice
1/4 cup red wine vinegar
1 tablespoon dried cumin
1 teaspoon tabasco
1 teaspoon pepper
1 teaspoon salt
(garnish) sour cream

Method:
1. Place onions, both peppers, cucumber and tomatoes in a food processor and purée.
2. In a large mixing bowl, combine purée, tomato juice, vinegar, cumin, Tabasco, pepper and salt. Mix well.
3. Refrigerate soup for about 24 hours.
4. Serve in a large soup crock and top with sour cream.

LOBSTER CORN CHOWDA

Serving size- 1 large soup crock

Ingredients:
1/4 cup butter
2 lbs all purpose potatoes (washed, peeled and finely diced)
1 small finely diced white onion
1 cup finely diced celery
1 cup canned whole kernel corn (drained)
1 cup fresh cooked lobster meat (chopped)
1/4 cup all purpose flour
3 cups vegetable broth
1 teaspoon celery salt
1 teaspoon pepper
1 teaspoon salt
1 cup heavy cream

Method:
1. Melt butter in a large stockpot over medium heat.
2. Sauté potatoes until just fork tender.
3. Add onion and celery and continue cooking fir 4-5 minutes stirring frequently.
4. Add corn, lobster and flour. Mix well.
5. Add vegetable broth and bring to a boil.
6. Add all other ingredients and lower heat to a simmer. Cook chowda for about 20 minutes.
7. Serve in a large soup crock.

Salsas

CHUNKY FRESH VEGETABLE SALSA

Serving size-1 party bowl

Ingredients:
2 cups finely diced plum tomatoes
1 large finely diced red onion
1 large finely diced red bell pepper
1 large finely diced green bell pepper
1 large finely diced orange bell pepper
2 tablespoons finely chopped fresh cilantro leaves
2 tablespoons dark chili powder
1 tablespoon dried cumin
1 1/2 cups tomato juice
1/4 cup lime juice
1 teaspoon pepper
1 teaspoon salt

Method:
1. Combine all ingredients in a large mixing bowl. Mix well.
2. Refrigerate mixture for about 2 hours.
3. Serve.

WARM CREAMY SWEET CORN SALSA

Serving size-1 party bowl

Ingredients:
2 tablespoons extra virgin olive oil
10 ears sweet corn on the cob (shucked)
1 large finely diced red bell pepper
1 large finely diced green bell pepper
1 large finely diced white onion
2 tablespoons finely chopped fresh parsley
2 tablespoons Cajun seasoning
1 1/2 cups heavy cream
1/2 teaspoon pepper
1/2 teaspoon salt

Method:
1. Hold ear of corn standing tall on a cutting board and run blade of knife down to remove corn kernels, repeat until all kernels are removed.
2. Drizzle olive oil in a large sauté pan over medium heat.
3. Sauté corn, red pepper, green pepper and white onion, stirring frequently for about 10 minutes.
4. Add parsley, Cajun seasoning, heavy cream, pepper and salt. Reduce until cream thickens.
5. Serve.

SPICY SHRIMP SALSA

Serving size-1 party bowl

Ingredients:
1 lb U31-35 white shrimp (cleaned, peeled and de-veined)
Ice water
1 tablespoon hot sauce
3 large finely diced vine ripened yellow tomatoes
3 large finely diced vine ripened red tomatoes
3 small finely diced jalapeño peppers
1 large finely diced red onion
2 tablespoons finely chopped fresh purple basil leaves
1 cup tomato juice
1/4 cup lemon juice
1/2 teaspoon extra virgin olive oil
1/2 teaspoon pepper
1/2 teaspoon salt

Method:
1. Bring pot of water to a boil, cook shrimp until nice and pink and the inside is white. Cool in ice water.
2. Dice the shrimp and place in a large mixing bowl with all other ingredients. Mix well.
3. Refrigerate mixture for about 2 hours.
4. Serve.

WHITE GASPACHO SALSA

Serving size - 1 party bowl

Ingredients:
2 large finely diced green bell peppers
2 cups finely diced green tomatoes
1 large finely diced white onion
1/2 cup fresh chopped scallions
1 large finely diced seedless cucumber (peeled)
1/2 cup finely diced celery
1/4 cup rice wine vinegar
1/2 cup extra virgin olive oil
2 tablespoons dried cumin
2 tablespoons finely chopped fresh cilantro leaves
1/2 cup lemon juice
1/2 teaspoon pepper
1/4 teaspoon salt

Method:
1. Combine all ingredients in a large mixing bowl. Mix well.
2. Refrigerate mixture for about 2 hours.
3. Serve.

 ## ITALIAN TOMATO SALSA

Serving size – 1 party bowl

Ingredients:
2 tablespoons extra virgin olive oil
1 large eggplant (peeled and diced)
3 cups finely diced plum tomatoes
1 large finely diced red onion
1 tablespoon fresh chopped garlic
1/2 cup tomato juice
1/4 cup extra virgin olive oil
2 tablespoons finely chopped fresh oregano leaves
1/4 cup balsamic vinegar
1/2 teaspoon pepper
1/4 teaspoon salt

Method:
1. Drizzle 2 tablespoons olive oil in a large sauté pan over medium heat.
2. Sauté eggplant for about 5-10 minutes until soft. Remove from heat and let cool.
3. Combine all other ingredients in a large mixing bowl. Add eggplant and mix well.
4. Refrigerate mixture for about 2 hours.
5. Serve.

CURRY SALSA

Serving size-1 party bowl

Ingredients:
1 large finely diced seedless cucumber (peeled)
2 cups finely diced plum tomatoes
1 large finely diced red bell pepper
1 large finely diced green bell pepper
1/2 cup fresh chopped scallions
1 large finely diced red onion
2 tablespoons mild curry paste
2 tablespoons tomato paste
5/4 cup tomato juice
1/4 cup extra virgin olive oil
1/2 teaspoon pepper
1/4 teaspoon salt

Method:
1. Combine all ingredients in a large mixing bowl. Mix well.
2. Refrigerate mixture for about 2 hours.
3. Serve.

BLACK BEAN SALSA

Serving size-1 party bowl

Ingredients:
1 large finely diced orange bell pepper
1 large finely diced green bell pepper
1 large finely diced red bell pepper
1 large finely diced yellow bell pepper
1 large finely diced jalapeño pepper
1 large finely diced red onion
2 (15 oz cans) black beans (drained)
2 tablespoons finely chopped fresh cilantro leaves
1/4 teaspoon crushed red pepper flakes
1 cup tomato juice
1/4 cup extra virgin olive oil
1/4 cup lemon juice
1/2 teaspoon pepper
1/2 teaspoon salt

Method:
1. Combine all ingredients in a large mixing bowl. Mix well.
2. Refrigerate for about 2 hours.
3. Serve.

PINEAPPLE SALSA

Serving size-1 party bowl

Ingredients:
1 large finely diced fresh pineapple
1/4 cup finely diced white onion
1/4 cup finely chopped fresh chives
1/4 cup finely diced plum tomatoes
2 tablespoons finely chopped fresh mint leaves
1/2 cup pineapple juice
1/4 cup tomato juice
1 tablespoon dark chili powder
1 tablespoon dried cumin
1/2 teaspoon pepper
1/4 teaspoon salt

Method:
1. Combine all ingredients in a large mixing bowl. Mix well.
2. Refrigerate for about 2 hours.
3. Serve.

Salads

MEDITERRANEAN TORTELLINI SALAD

Serving size-1 party bowl

Ingredients:
2 small bags frozen cheese tortellini
1 cup finely diced plum tomatoes
1 large finely diced green bell pepper
1 large finely diced red bell pepper
1 large finely diced red onion
8 oz bag baby spinach leaves (chopped)
1 tablespoons capers
8 oz crumbled feta cheese
1 teaspoon fresh chopped garlic
3/4 cup extra virgin olive oil
1/4 cup red wine vinegar
1 teaspoon pepper

Method:
1. Bring pot of water to a boil. Cook tortellini until fork tender. Drain and cool.
2. In a large mixing bowl, combine cooled tortellini and all other ingredients, one at a time. Mix well.
3. Refrigerate salad for about 4 hours.
4. Serve.

CHILLED SPANISH RICE SALAD

Serving size-1 party bowl

Ingredients:
6 cups water
3 cups white rice (long grain)
1/2 cup canned crushed tomatoes
1/2 cup mayonnaise
1 cup canned green olives (chopped)
1 cup canned black olives (chopped)
1 cup canned pimentos (chopped)
1 cup finely diced plum tomatoes
1/2 cup finely diced red onion
2 tablespoons dark chili powder
1 tablespoon dried cumin
1/2 teaspoon pepper
1/2 teaspoon salt

Method:
1. In a pot, bring water to a boil. Add rice and reduce heat to a simmer and cover, stirring occasionally. Cook until tender and all water is absorbed. Remove from heat and cool.
2. In a large mixing bowl, combine cooled rice and all other ingredients, one at a time. Mix well.
3. Refrigerate salad for about 4 hours.
4. Serve

BLUE CHEESE POTATO SALAD

Serving size-1 party bowl

Ingredients:
3 lbs red bliss potatoes (washed & quartered)
1/2 cup mayonnaise
1 cup crumbled blue cheese
1/4 cup red wine vinegar
1/2 cup chopped cooked bacon
1/2 cup fresh chopped scallions
1 teaspoon paprika
1/2 teaspoon pepper
1/2 teaspoon salt

Method:
1. Place potatoes in a pot and fill with cold water. Boil potatoes until fork tender. Drain and cool.
2. In a large mixing bowl, combine cooled potatoes and all other ingredients one at a time. Mix well.
3. Refrigerate salad for about 4 hours.
4. Serve.

MARGARITA SALAD

Serving size-1 party bowl

Ingredients:
3 cups fresh mozzarella cheese (ciligiene)
3 cups cherry tomatoes
3 cups yellow cherry tomatoes
1 cup finely diced red onion
2 tablespoons finely chopped fresh purple basil leaves
2 tablespoons finely chopped fresh basil leaves
1/2 cup extra virgin olive oil
2 tablespoons lime juice
1/2 teaspoon pepper
1/4 teaspoon salt

Method:
1. In a large mixing bowl, combine all ingredients. Mix well.
2. Refrigerate salad for about 24 hours.
3. Serve.

BAKED POTATO SALAD

Serving size-1 party bowl

Ingredients:
3 lbs all-purpose potatoes (washed)
1/4 cup finely chopped fresh chives
2 tablespoons mayonnaise
1/4 cup sour cream
1/4 cup red wine vinegar
1/2 cup chopped cooked bacon
1 tablespoon paprika
1/2 teaspoon pepper
1/2 teaspoon salt

Method:
1. Cut potatoes into a large diced size.
2. Place potatoes in a pot and fill with cold water. Boil potatoes until fork tender. Drain and cool.
3. In a large mixing bowl, combine cooled potatoes and all other ingredients, one at a time. Mix well.
4. Refrigerate salad for about 4 hours.
5. Serve.

 # SWEET POTATO SALAD

Serving size-1 party bowl

Ingredients:
3 lbs sweet potatoes (washed & diced)
3/4 cup finely diced red onion
2 tablespoons finely chopped fresh parsley
1/2 cup chopped cooked bacon
1 tablespoon finely chopped rosemary leaves
1/4 cup apple cider vinegar
1/2 cup mayonnaise
1/2 teaspoon pepper
1/2 teaspoon salt

Method:
1. Place potatoes in a pot and fill with cold water. Boil potatoes until fork tender. Drain and cool.
2. In a large mixing bowl, combine cooled potatoes and all other ingredients together. Mix well.
3. Refrigerate salad for about 4 hours.
4. Serve.

BARRY'S FAVORITE BLUE CHEESE DRESSING

Serving size-1 large bottle of dressing

Ingredients:
1/2 cup mayonnaise
16 oz cream cheese (softened)
1 cup sour cream
8 oz crumbled blue cheese
1/4 cup red wine vinegar
1 tablespoon Dijon mustard
2 tablespoons milk
1 teaspoon granulated garlic
1 tablespoon finely chopped fresh parsley
1/2 teaspoon pepper
1/2 teaspoon salt

Method:
1. In a large mixing bowl, beat mayonnaise, cream cheese and sour cream together until smooth and creamy.
2. Add all other ingredients one at a time. Mix well.
3. Refrigerate dressing for at least 24 hours.
4. Serve.

CHILLED BROCCOFLOWER SALAD

Serving size 1 party bowl

Ingredients:
2 large heads broccoflower
1/4 cup mayonnaise
1/4 cup finely diced red onions
1 cup finely diced plum tomatoes
2 tablespoons rice wine vinegar
2 tablespoons finely chopped fresh parsley
2 tablespoon finely chopped fresh basil leaves
1/2 teaspoon pepper
1/4 teaspoon salt

Method:
1. Cut heads of broccoflower into " diced size pieces.
2. Bring pot of water to a boil. Cook broccoflower until fork tender. Drain and cool under cold water. Leave in colander to drain for about 10 minutes.
3. In a large mixing bowl, combine broccoflower and all other ingredients, one at a time. Mix well.
4. Refrigerate salad for about 24 hours.
5. Serve.

CAJUN POTATO SALAD

Serving size-1 party bowl

Ingredients:
3 lbs red bliss potatoes (washed & quartered)
1/2 cup finely diced red onion
1/2 cup canned roasted red peppers (finely diced)
1/2 cup fresh chopped scallions
1/2 cup mayonnaise
1/4 cup red wine vinegar
2 tablespoons Cajun seasoning
1/2 teaspoon pepper
1/4 teaspoon salt

Method:
1. Place potatoes in a pot and fill with cold water. Boil potatoes until fork tender. Drain and cool.
2. In a large mixing bowl, combine cooled potatoes and all other ingredients one at a time. Mix well.
3. Refrigerate salad for about 4 hours.
4. Serve.

GARDEN VEGGIE SLAW

Serving size-1 party bowl

Ingredients:
1/2 head green cabbage (shredded)
1/2 head red cabbage (shredded)
3 large carrots (peeled and shredded)
1/2 cup fresh chopped scallions
1 large finely sliced white onion
2 medium zucchini (julienne)
2 medium summer squash (julienne)
3/4 cup mayonnaise
1/2 cup rice wine vinegar
2 tablespoons finely chopped fresh parsley
1/2 teaspoon pepper
1/2 teaspoon salt

Method:
1. In a large mixing bowl, combine all ingredients one at a time. Mix well.
2. Refrigerate slaw for about 4 hours.
3. Serve.

SPICY BELL PEPPER SLAW

Serving size-1 party bowl

Ingredients:
1/2 head green cabbage (shredded)
2 large red bell peppers (julienne)
2 large green bell peppers (julienne)
2 large orange bell peppers (julienne)
2 large yellow bell peppers (julienne)
2 pinch's crushed red pepper flakes
1/2 cup mayonnaise
1/4 cup red wine vinegar
1 tablespoon paprika
1 teaspoon pepper
1 teaspoon salt

Method:
1. In a large mixing bowl, combine all ingredients, one at a time. Mix well.
2. Refrigerate slaw for about 4 hours.
3. Serve.

RED, WHITE AND BLUE THREE BEAN SALAD

Serving size-1 party bowl

Ingredients:
2 cups canned dark red kidney beans (drained)
2 cups canned navy beans (drained)
2 cups canned cannelloni beans (drained)
1 tablespoon fresh chopped garlic
1/4 cup heavy cream
1/2 cup mayonnaise
1/4 cup finely chopped fresh basil leaves
1/2 cup finely diced plum tomatoes
1/2 teaspoon pepper
1/2 teaspoon salt

Method:
1. Combine all ingredients in a large mixing bowl, one at a time. Mix well.
2. Refrigerate salad for about 2 hours.
3. Serve.

APPLE COLESLAW

Serving size-1 party bowl

Ingredients:
6 golden delicious apples (julienne)
6 red delicious apples (julienne)
1/2 cup mayonnaise
1/4 cup apple cider vinegar
1/4 cup fresh chopped scallions
1/4 cup dried cranberries
2 tablespoons finely chopped fresh parsley
1/2 teaspoon pepper
1/2 teaspoon salt

Method:
1. Combine apples and mayonnaise in a large mixing bowl. Add vinegar, scallions, cranberries, parsley, pepper and salt. Mix well.
2. Refrigerate coleslaw for about 2 hours.
3. Serve.

FUNNY BONE SALAD

Serving size-1 party bowl

Ingredients:
2 tablespoons vegetable oil
1 pinch salt
1 lb box dried elbow macaroni
1/2 cup mayonnaise
1 tablespoon extra virgin oil
1 tablespoon Dijon mustard
1/2 cup fresh chopped scallions
1/2 cup finely diced white onion
1/4 cup rice wine vinegar
1/2 teaspoon pepper
1/2 teaspoon salt

Method:
1. Bring pot of water to a boil. Drizzle vegetable oil and pinch of salt in water. Cook elbow macaroni until just tender. Drain and cool under cold water. Leave in colander to drain for about 10 minutes.
2. In a large mixing bowl, combine cooled macaroni and all other ingredients, one at a time. Mix well.
3. Refrigerate salad for about 4 hours.
4. Serve.

PASTA COBB SALAD

Serving size-1 party bowl

Ingredients:
2 tablespoons vegetable oil
1 pinch salt
1 lb box dried fusilli pasta
1 cup finely diced plum tomatoes
1/2 cup chopped cooked bacon
2 large fresh avocados (skin removed & diced)
8 large hard-boiled eggs (chilled & chopped)
8 oz crumbled blue cheese
3/4 cup extra virgin olive oil
1/4 cup red wine vinegar
2 tablespoons finely chopped fresh parsley
1/2 teaspoon pepper
1/2 teaspoon salt

Method:
1. Bring pot of water to a boil, drizzle 2 tablespoons of vegetable oil and a pinch of salt into water. Cook fusilli until just tender. Drain and cool under cold water. Leave in colander to drain for about 10 minutes.
2. In a large mixing bowl, combine cooled pasta, tomatoes, red onion, bacon and avocados. Mix well.
3. Fold in all other ingredients one at a time.
4. Refrigerate salad for about 4 hours.
5. Serve.

CALAMARI FRA DIAVLO SALAD

Serving size-1 party bowl

Ingredients:
2 lbs calamari (tubes only)
1 small diced red bell pepper
1 small diced green bell pepper
1 small diced yellow bell pepper
1 small diced orange bell pepper
3 large diced vine ripened red tomatoes
1 large finely diced red onion
1 cup tomato juice
2 tablespoons extra virgin olive oil
1/4 cup red wine vinegar
1 teaspoon Tabasco
1 pinch crushed red pepper flakes
1/2 teaspoon pepper
1/2 teaspoon salt
1 large head of romaine lettuce (washed & chopped)
1/2 cup grated Romano cheese

Method:
1. Cut calamari tubes into 1/2" rings.
2. Bring pot of water to a boil. Cook calamari for about 1 minute, stirring constantly. Make sure you don't over cook calamari. Over cooked calamari is very chewy and tough. You want it to be nice and tender. Drain and cool under cold water. Leave in colander to drain for about 10 minutes.
3. In a large mixing bowl, combine cooled calamari and all other ingredients, one at a time, except romaine lettuce and Romano cheese. Mix well.
4. Place chopped romaine lettuce in a large serving bowl, top with calamari salad mixture and sprinkle with Romano cheese.
5. Refrigerate salad for about 4 hours.
6. Serve.

TUNA SALAD LETTUCE WRAPS

Serving size- 1 party platter, 15 wraps

Ingredients:
30 ozs canned tuna in water (drained)
1/4 cup mayonnaise
2 tablespoons lemon juice
1 tablespoon capers
1/2 cup finely diced red onion
2 tablespoons finely chopped fresh parsley
1/2 teaspoon pepper
1/4 teaspoon salt
15 bibb lettuce leaves (washed & patted dry)
3 tablespoons extra virgin olive oil
1 teaspoon red wine vinegar
1 teaspoon honey

Method:
1. In a large mixing bowl, combine tuna, mayonnaise, lemon juice, capers, red onion, parsley, pepper and salt. Mix well.
2. Stuff each lettuce leaf with equal amounts of tuna salad mixture, arrange stuffed lettuce leaves on a serving platter.
3. In a small mixing bowl, combine extra virgin olive oil, vinegar and honey. Mix well. Drizzle over stuffed lettuce leaves.
4. Refrigerate platter for about 1 hour.
5. Serve.

ORZO CONFETTI PASTA SALAD

Serving size-1 party bowl

Ingredients:
4 cups dried orzo pasta
1 large finely diced red bell pepper
1 large finely diced yellow bell pepper
1 large finely diced green bell pepper
1 cup finely diced plum tomatoes
1 large finely diced red onion
8 oz bag baby spinach leaves (chopped)
1 teaspoon fresh chopped garlic
3/4 cup extra virgin olive oil
1/4 cup red wine vinegar
1/2 teaspoon pepper
1/2 teaspoon salt

Method:
1. Bring pot of water to a boil, drizzle vegetable oil and pinch of salt into water. Cook orzo pasta until large and tender. Drain and cool under cold water. Leave in colander to drain for about 10 minutes.
2. In a large mixing bowl, combine cooled orzo and all other ingredients, one at a time. Mix well.
3. Refrigerate salad for about 4 hours.
4. Serve.

CHIPOTLE CHICKEN SALAD FRISBEE'S

Serving size- 1 party platter, 6 frisbee's

Ingredients:
2 lbs grilled boneless chicken breast (chilled & diced)
1/2 cup mayonnaise
1 tablespoon finely chopped canned chipotle peppers
1/4 cup fresh chopped scallions
1 tablespoon lime juice
1/2 teaspoon pepper
1/2 teaspoon salt
6 4" pita bread
1/2 head iceberg lettuce (shredded)
2 large diced vine ripened red tomatoes
1 small finely diced red onion

Method:
1. In a large mixing bowl, combine diced chicken, mayonnaise, chipotle peppers, scallions, lime juice, pepper and salt. Mix well.
2. Place pita bread on a serving platter and top with equal amounts of shredded lettuce, chicken salad, diced tomatoes and red onion.
3. Serve.

# CHERRY TOMATO AND MOZZARELLA KEBOBS

Serving size-1 party platter, 20 kebobs

Ingredients:
20 6" wooden skewers
40 cherry tomatoes
40 fresh mozzarella cheese balls (ciligiene)
1 large head romaine lettuce (washed and chopped)
1/2 cup extra virgin olive oil
2 tablespoons balsamic vinegar
2 tablespoons finely chopped fresh basil leaves

Method:
1. Place two cherry tomatoes and two mozzarella balls on each skewer.
2. Arrange skewers on a serving platter of chopped romaine lettuce.
3. In a small mixing bowl, combine olive oil, vinegar and basil. Mix well.
4. Drizzle over skewers and romaine leaves
5. Refrigerate platter for about 1 hour.
6. Serve.

GREEK SALAD WITH FRIED EGGPLANT CROUTONS

Serving size-1 party platter

Ingredients:
1 large eggplant (peeled & diced to 3/4")
1 cup all purpose flour
2 large eggs
1 cup milk
1 cup unseasoned breadcrumbs
Oil for frying
1 tablespoon granulated garlic
1 large head romaine lettuce (washed & chopped)
3 large sliced vine ripened red tomatoes
1 large finely sliced red onion
8 oz crumbled feta cheese
3/4 cup canned sliced black Spanish olives (drained)
1 tablespoon fresh chopped garlic
3/4 cup extra virgin olive oil
1/4 cup red wine vinegar
1/4 teaspoon pepper

Method:
1. Coat eggplant in flour.
2. In a large mixing bowl, beat eggs and milk together.
3. Dredge floured eggplant in egg mixture.
4. Coat in breadcrumbs.
5. Pour oil in a large stockpot until 1/2 full and heat to 370°F.
6. Fry eggplant until golden brown and tender inside. Remove from oil, pat dry and season with granulated garlic. Set aside.
7. Place chopped greens on a platter, top with tomatoes, red onion, feta cheese, black olives and eggplant croutons.
8. In a small mixing bowl, combine, garlic, olive oil, vinegar and pepper. Mix well and drizzle over platter of salad.
9. Serve.

CHILLED GRILLED ZUCCHINI SALAD

Serving size-1 party bowl

Ingredients:
3 large zucchini (sliced on an angle 1/2")
1/2 cup vegetable oil
2 tablespoon dried oregano
1 large finely diced red bell pepper
1 large finely diced red onion
1 cup finely diced plum tomatoes
2 tablespoons finely chopped fresh basil leaves
1 teaspoon fresh chopped garlic
1/4 cup extra virgin olive oil
3 tablespoons balsamic vinegar
1/2 teaspoon pepper
1/2 teaspoon salt
1/2 cup shredded Parmesan cheese

Method:
1. In a large mixing bowl, combine zucchini, vegetable oil and oregano. Mix well and let sit for about 1 hour.
2. Pre-heat grill to a medium heat, grill zucchini for about 3 minutes on each side until fork tender. Remove from heat and cool for about 1 hour in refrigerator.
3. In a large mixing bowl, combine cooled zucchini and all other ingredients, one at a time. Mix well.
4. Refrigerate salad for about 2 hours.
5. Serve.

CHILLED POTATO AND GREEN BEAN SALAD

Serving size-1 party bowl

Ingredients:
2 lbs red bliss potatoes (washed & quartered)
2 lbs fresh green beans (stems removed)
ice water
1/2 cup finely diced red onion
1/2 cup chopped cooked bacon
6 large hard-boiled eggs (chilled & chopped)
1/4 cup extra virgin olive oil
3 tablespoons red wine vinegar
1/2 teaspoon pepper
1/2 teaspoon salt

Method:
1. Place potatoes in a pot and fill with cold water. Boil potatoes until fork tender. Drain and cool.
2. Bring pot of water to a boil. Cook green beans for about 4 minutes until nice bright green. Drain and place green beans in ice water until cool. Remove beans from ice water and pat dry.
3. In a large mixing bowl, combine cooled potatoes, green beans and all other ingredients one at a time. Mix well.
4. Refrigerate salad for about 4 hours.
5. Serve.

Starters

POTATO & SOUR CREAM MONEY BAGS

Serving size- 6 bags

Ingredients:
1 lb red bliss potatoes (washed)
1 tablespoon butter
1/4 cup heavy cream
1/4 cup fresh chopped scallions
2 pinch's pepper
1 pinch salt
1/4 cup sour cream
1 sheet thawed puff pastry (store bought)
cooking spray
1 large egg (beaten)

Method:
1. Pre-heat oven 400°F.
2. Place potatoes in a pot and fill with cold water. Boil potatoes until fork tender. Drain and cool.
3. In a large mixing bowl, mash the potatoes, butter, heavy cream, scallions, pepper, salt and sour cream together until smooth and creamy.
4. Cut puff pastry into 6 equal squares. Scoop equal portions of potato mixture in the center of all 6 pastry squares.
5. Pull all 4 corners of pastry up over the center of the potatoes and pinch pastry together. Twist the top of the pastry to form a moneybag.
6. Place money bags on sprayed baking sheet. Brush each pastry with beaten egg and bake for about 30-35 minutes or until golden brown.
7. Serve.

PORQUPINE POTATO CROQUETS

Serving size - 1 party platter

Ingredients:
2 lbs red bliss potatoes (washed & quartered)
oil for frying
1/2 cup finely chopped fresh chives
1/2 cup all purpose flour
2 large eggs
1 teaspoon pepper
1 teaspoon salt
3/4 cup unbleached flour
3 large eggs
1 cup 1/2 & 1/2
1 cup potato sticks (store bought)
1 cup unseasoned breadcrumbs
(garnish) sour cream

Method:
1. Place potatoes in a pot and fill with cold water. Boil potatoes until fork tender. Drain and cool.
2. Pour oil in large stock pot until 1/2 full and heat to 370°F.
3. In a large mixing bowl, mash cooled potatoes, chives, all purpose flour, eggs, pepper and salt. Mix well.
4. Form golf ball size croquets with equal amounts of potato mixture.
5. Coat potatoes in unbleached flour.
6. In a small mixing bowl, beat eggs and cream together. Mix well.
7. In another small bowl, crush potato sticks, add breadcrumbs and mix together.
8. One at a time, dip the croquets in egg mixture and then in breadcrumb mixture.
9. Fry croquets for about 5 minutes, remove from oil and pat dry.
10. Serve with sour cream.

# GUINNESS BATTERED CHICKEN FINGERS

Serving size- 1 party platter

Ingredients:
1 lbs boneless skinless chicken breast (cut into strips)
oil for frying
1 cup unbleached flour
1 teaspoon baking powder
3 large eggs
1 can Guinness
1 tablespoon finely chopped fresh parsley
1 tablespoon Dijon mustard
1 pinch pepper
1 pinch salt
1 cup all-purpose flour

Method:
1. Pour water in a large stockpot until 1/2 full and bring to a boil. Lower the heat to a simmer.
2. Poach the chicken strips for about 8-10 minutes. Remove and pat dry.
3. Pour oil in a large stockpot until 1/2 full and heat to 370°F.
4. In a large mixing bowl, combine unbleached four, baking powder, eggs, Guinness, parsley, mustard, pepper and salt. Mix well.
5. Coat chicken stripes with all-purpose flour. Dip each strip in Guinness batter and fry for about 3-5 minutes until crispy and golden brown. Remove from the oil and pat dry.
6. Serve.

ORANGE CURRY CHICKEN WINGS

Serving size- 20 wings

Ingredients:
oil for frying
20 chicken wings (rinsed under cold water and patted dry)
1/2 cup orange juice
1 tablespoon cold water
1 cup orange marmalade (store bought)
1 tablespoon mild curry paste
1 pinch pepper
1 pinch salt
1 tablespoon finely chopped fresh parsley
1/4 cup fresh chopped scallions

Method:
1. Pour oil in a large stockpot until 1/2 full and heat to 370°F.
2. Fry chicken wings for about 8-10 minutes. Remove from oil and pat dry.
3. In a large mixing bowl, combine all other ingredients. Mix well. Add chicken wings to mixing bowl and coat well.
4. Place wings on baking sheet and bake for about 20 minutes.
5. Serve.

SMOKED SALMON WRAPPED SEA SCALLOPS
(with a lemon dill sour cream)

Serving size- 1 party platter, 15 scallops

Ingredients:
2 tablespoons extra virgin olive oil
15 U-10 jumbo sea scallops (picked)
1/4 cup all-purpose flour
1/4 teaspoon pepper
1/4 teaspoon salt
15 slices smoked salmon
(garnish) lemon wedges

Method:
1. Drizzle olive oil in a large skillet over medium heat.
2. In a large mixing bowl, combine scallops, flour, pepper and salt. Mix well.
3. Remove any excess flour from scallops. Sauté scallops for about 4 minutes, then turn scallops over and sauté for another 4 minutes. Remove from heat and let cool for about 3 minutes.
4. Wrap each scallop with a slice of smoked salmon and serve with lemon dill sour cream and lemon wedges.

Lemon dill sour cream
1 tablespoon finely chopped fresh dill
3/4 cup sour cream
2 tablespoons lemon juice
2 pinch's pepper
1 pinch salt

1. In a large mixing bowl, combine all ingredients. Mix well.
2. Refrigerate for about 1 hour.
3. Serve.

EASY PULLED PORK QUESADILLA'S

Serving size-1 party platter, about 15-20 pieces

Ingredients:
1 1/2 lbs pork tenderloin (trimmed)
1/2 teaspoon dark chili powder
1/4 teaspoon dried cumin
1/2 teaspoon garlic powder
1/2 teaspoon onion powder
1 tablespoon extra virgin olive oil
4 12" flour tortillas
1 tablespoon ketchup
1/4 cup Dijon mustard
1/2 cup fresh chopped scallions
1/2 cup shredded cheddar cheese
1/2 cup shredded Monterey-jack cheese

Method:
1. Pre-heat oven 400°F.
2. In a small mixing bowl, combine chili powder, cumin, garlic powder and onion powder. Mix well. Place tenderloin in mixing bowl and coat well.
3. Place tenderloin in a baking dish and drizzle with olive oil. Bake for about 35-40 minutes. Remove from oven. While meat is still warm, pull the strips of pork apart. Set aside to cool.
4. Lower oven temperature to 300°F.
5. In a small mixing bowl, mix ketchup and Dijon mustard together and spread mixture evenly over the 4 tortillas.
6. In another small mixing bowl, combine scallions, cheddar cheese and Monterey-jack cheese together and divide the mixture equally over the tortillas. Spread pork evenly over the cheese mixture and fold tortillas in half.
7. Place on a baking sheet and bake for about 10-12 minutes, until tortillas are brown and crispy. Cut tortillas into 4 or 5 pieces.
8. Serve.

PRETZEL CRUSTED CRABCAKES
(with a dijon horseradish sauce)

Serving size- 1 party platter, 12 cakes

Ingredients:
3 tablespoons extra virgin olive oil
1 lbs fresh lump crabmeat
4 large eggs
1 1/2 cup mayonnaise
1/2 cup all purpose flour
8 slices white sandwich bread (crust removed and diced)
1 tablespoon Dijon mustard
1/2 cup panko breadcrumbs
1 tablespoon lemon juice
1/2 teaspoon pepper
1/2 teaspoon salt
2 cups ground pretzels (unsalted)

Method:
1. Pre-heat oven to 350°F.
2. Drizzle olive oil in a large skillet over medium heat.
3. In a large mixing bowl, combine all ingredients except ground pretzels. Mix well. Divide mixture into 12 equal portions and form into round cakes.
4. Coat each cake with ground pretzels and sauté for about 4 minutes. Turn cakes over and place skillet in oven for about 15 minutes.
5. Serve with Dijon horseradish sauce

Dijon horseradish sauce.

1 tablespoon prepared horseradish
2 tablespoons Dijon mustard
1 cup sour cream
1/2 cup mayonnaise
1/4 cup milk
2 tablespoons finely chopped fresh chives
1/4 teaspoon pepper
1/4 teaspoon salt

Method:
1. In a small mixing bowl, combine all ingredients. Mix well.
2. Refrigerate for about 1 hour.
3. Serve.

# SPICY BAKED BEEF TAQUITOS

Serving size- 1 party platter-12 taquitos

Ingredients:
2 tablespoons extra virgin olive oil
1 large finely diced red onion
1 1/2 lbs ground beef (85% lean)
4 tablespoons tomato paste
2 tablespoons dark chili powder
2 tablespoons dried cumin
1 teaspoon Tabasco
12 6" flour tortillas
1 cup shredded pepper jack cheese
24 toothpicks
cooking spray
(garnish) sour cream

Method:
1. Preheat oven to 400°F.
2. Drizzle olive oil in a large skillet over medium heat.
3. Sauté onion for about 2 minutes stirring occasionally, add ground beef and continue cooking and stirring for 10-12 minutes until all beef is cooked.
4. Add tomato paste, chili powder, cumin and Tabasco to the beef mixture. Mix well. Remove from heat.
5. Divide shredded cheese equally over tortillas, spread ground beef mixture evenly over cheese. Roll each tortilla tightly, place toothpick through top and bottom of tortillas.
6. Place taquitos on a sprayed baking sheet and bake for about 10-15 minutes until golden brown and crispy.
7. Serve with sour cream.

ROAST BEEF WRAPPED ASPARAGUS SPEARS
(with Boursin cheese)

Serving size- 1 party platter, 12 wraps

Ingredients:
24 large asparagus spears
ice water
12 slices rare deli roast beef
1 cup boursin cheese

Method:
1. Bring pot of water to a boil.
2. Cut off 1 1/2 to 2" from the bottom of each asparagus spear. Cook spears in water for about 5 minutes, make sure they have a nice green color to them. Remove from the hot water and place in ice water.
3. Cool for about 10 minutes. Remove from ice water and pat dry.
4. Spread boursin cheese evenly on each slice of roast beef. Place two asparagus spears in the center of each slice of roast beef and roll them nice and tight.
5. Refrigerate for about 1 hour.
6. Serve.

FRIED ZUCCHINI SPEARS

Serving size- 1 party platter

Ingredients:
oil for frying
3 large zucchini (peeled and cut into 3/4" spears)
1 cup unbleached flour
4 large eggs
2 cups 1/2 & 1/2
1 tablespoon dried oregano
1 tablespoon garlic powder
1 tablespoon onion powder
1 teaspoon pepper
1 teaspoon salt
2 cups unseasoned breadcrumbs

Method:
1. Pour oil in a large stockpot until 1/2 full and heat to 370°F.
2. Coat zucchini spears with unbleached flour. Set aside.
3. In a large mixing bowl, beat eggs, 1/2 & 1/2, oregano, garlic powder, onion powder, pepper and salt.
4. Place zucchini in mixing bowl with egg mixture and coat well.
5. Remove zucchini and coat each spear with breadcrumbs.
6. Fry the spears for about 8 minutes until crisp outside and tender inside. Remove from oil and pat dry.
7. Serve.

CREAMY CHEDDAR CHICKEN NACHOS

Serving size- 1 party bowl

Ingredients:
2 tablespoons butter
2 lbs boneless skinless chicken breast (diced)
1 large finely diced green bell pepper
1 large finely diced red onion
1/4 cup all-purpose flour
1 tablespoon dark chili powder
1 tablespoon cumin
1 cup heavy cream
1 cup shredded cheddar cheese
1/2 teaspoon pepper
1/2 teaspoon salt.
(garnish) 1 bag round nacho corn chips (store bought)

Method:
1. In a large skillet over medium heat, melt butter and sauté diced chicken, stir occasionally. Cook for about 8-10 minutes. Add peppers and red onion and cook for about another 5 minutes stirring frequently.
2. Add flour, chili powder and cumin to the skillet. Mix well and cook for about 40 seconds.
3. Whisk heavy cream into skillet and reduce the cream until it starts to thicken. Turn off heat and add cheese, pepper and salt. Mix well.
4. Place nachos on platter and top with cheddar cheese mixture.
5. Serve.

# OLD FASHIONED FRIED VIDALIA ONION RINGS

Serving size- 1 party basket

Ingredients:
oil for frying
3 large sweet Vidalia onions (peeled and thinly sliced into rings)
2 cups unbleached flour
1 tablespoon granulated garlic
1/4 cup finely chopped fresh parsley
4 large eggs
2 cups 1/2 & 1/2
1/2 teaspoon salt

Method:
1. Pour oil in a large stockpot until 1/2 full and heat to 370°F.
2. In a large mixing bowl, combine flour, granulated garlic and parsley.
3. Coat onion rings in flour mixture.
4. In another large mixing bowl, beat eggs and 1/2 & 1/2.
5. Dip onion rings into egg mixture and then coat with flour mixture. Shake off excess flour.
6. Fry rings for about 3-5 minutes until crispy and golden brown. Remove from oil and pat dry. Season with salt.
7. Serve.

CHILI PEPPER CRAB DIP
(with fried tortilla chips)

Serving size- 1 party casserole

Ingredients:
oil for frying
6 12" flour tortillas (cut into 2" triangle pieces)
2 lbs fresh lump crabmeat
8 oz cream cheese (softened)
1/2 cup fresh chopped scallions
2 small finely diced chili peppers
1 tablespoon dried cumin
2 tablespoons finely chopped fresh cilantro leaves
1 cup shredded cheddar cheese
1/4 teaspoon pepper
1/4 teaspoon salt

Method:
1. Pre-heat oven 350ºF.
2. Pour oil in a large stockpot until 1/2 full and heat to 370ºF.
3. Fry tortillas for about 3-5 minutes until crispy and golden brown, remove from oil and pat dry.
4. In a large mixing bowl, combine all other ingredients. Mix well.
5. Bake crab mixture in a casserole dish for about 30-35 minutes.
6. Serve with tortillas.

# PEEL AND EAT SHRIMP MARTINI

Serving size- 1 large martini glass

Ingredients:
2 tablespoons extra virgin olive oil
1 lb U31-40 white shrimp
1/2 cup finely diced plum tomatoes
1/4 cup vodka
1/4 cup tomato juice
1 pinch crushed red pepper flakes
1 tablespoon finely chopped fresh parsley
1/4 teaspoon pepper
1/4 teaspoon salt

Method:
1. Drizzle olive oil in a large skillet over medium heat.
2. Sauté shrimp until nice pink color forms under the shell, add tomatoes and stir for about 2 minutes. Pull skillet away from burner and add vodka. Place skillet back on burner and continue to cook for about 4-5 minutes. Add all other ingredients.
3. Toss and serve in a large martini glass.

BAKED STUFFED MUSHROOMS

Serving size- 1 party platter, 20 mushrooms

Ingredients:
1/4 cup extra virgin olive oil
1/2 cup finely diced white onion
1 1/2 lbs ground pork
1 tablespoon finely chopped fresh rosemary leaves
1/4 cup grated romano cheese
2 large eggs
1/2 cup unseasoned breadcrumbs
1/4 teaspoon pepper
1/4 teaspoon salt
20 large mushrooms (stems removed)

Method:
1. Preheat oven 350°F.
2. Drizzle olive oil in a large skillet over medium heat.
3. Sauté onions for 2 minutes stirring occasionally. Add ground pork and continue cooking and stirring for about 10-12 minutes until all the pork is cooked. Remove from heat and cool.
4. In a large mixing bowl, combine pork, rosemary, cheese, eggs, breadcrumbs, pepper and salt. Mix well.
5. Stuff each mushroom cap with equal amounts of stuffing. Place on a baking sheet and bake for about 35-40 minutes.
6. Serve.

ASIAN CABBAGE POT STICKERS

Serving size- 1 party platter, 15 stickers

Ingredients:
2 tablespoons sesame oil
1 small finely diced red bell pepper
1 head napa cabbage (shredded)
2 pinch's pepper
1 pinch salt
3 tablespoons extra virgin olive oil
15 round egg roll wrappers
3 large eggs (beaten)

Methods:
1. Drizzle sesame oil in a large skillet over medium heat.
2. Sauté peppers for 2 minutes stirring occasionally. Add cabbage, pepper and salt and continue cooking and stirring for about 3 minutes. Remove from heat and let cool.
3. Drizzle olive oil in a large skillet over medium heat.
4. Brush beaten eggs over the top of wontons. Scoop equal amounts of cabbage mixture in center of wontons. Fold one side of the wontons to the other to form a half moon. Press down firmly on edges of wontons.
5. Place wontons flat in skillet and cook for about 2 minutes. Turn over and cook for another 2 minutes until golden brown and the dough almost sticks to the pan.
6. Serve.

SAUCEY MEATBALLS

Serving size- 1 party casserole, 20 large meatballs

Ingredients:

Meatballs
1/4 cup extra virgin olive oil
1 lb ground pork
1 lb ground beef
1 lb ground veal
2 large finely diced white onions
2 tablespoons fresh chopped garlic
3 tablespoons dried oregano
8 slices white sandwich bread (crust removed and diced)
1 tablespoon garlic powder
1 teaspoon pepper
1 teaspoon salt

Method:
1. Preheat oven 375°F.
2. Drizzle olive oil in a skillet over medium-high heat.
3. In a large mixing bowl, combine all ingredients. Mix well.
4. Divide mixture into 20 equal portions. Roll each portion into a giant meatball.
5. Cook meatballs for about 5 minutes, turn meatballs and place skillet in oven and bake for about 20-25 minutes. Remove from oven and put in a casserole dish. Cover with sauce and bake for another 20 minutes.
6. Serve.

SAUCE
1/2 cup extra virgin olive oil
1 tablespoon fresh chopped garlic
1 tablespoon anchovy paste
4 cups canned crushed tomatoes
1/4 cup oregano
2 tablespoons garlic powder
1-teaspoon pepper
1-teaspoon salt

Method:
1. In a large mixing bowl, combine all ingredients. Mix well.

# CRAB AND LEEK RANGOONS

Serving size- 1 party platter, 20 rangoons

Ingredients:
oil for frying
2 tablespoons extra virgin olive oil
1 cup diced leeks (washed and dried)
1 lb fresh lump crabmeat
3 oz cream cheese (softened)
2 pinch's pepper
1 pinch salt
20 wonton wrappers
3 large eggs (beaten)

Method:
1. Pour oil in a large stockpot until 1/2 full and heat to 370°F.
2. Drizzle olive oil in a large skillet over medium heat.
3. Sauté leeks for about 5 minutes stirring occasionally. Add crab and cream cheese and continue cooking and stirring until cream cheese is well blended into crab and leek mixture. Season with pepper and salt. Remove from heat and cool.
4. Brush beaten eggs over the top of the wontons. Scoop equal amounts of crab mixture in center of wontons. Fold corner of wontons to the other corner to form a triangle. Press down firmly on edges of wontons.
5. Fry wontons for about 4-5 minutes until golden brown and crispy. Remove from oil and pat dry.
6. Serve.

FIRE CRACKER PIZZA STICKS
(With a chilled tomato dipping sauce)

Serving size- 1 party platter, 15 sticks

Ingredients:
oil for frying
15 egg roll wrappers
1 lb sliced pepperoni (chopped)
1 cup shredded Monterey jack cheese
1 cup shredded cheddar cheese
1 tablespoon dried oregano
1-teaspoon onion powder
1-teaspoon garlic powder
3 large eggs (beaten)

Method:
1. Pour oil in a large stockpot until 1/2 full and heat to 370°F.
2. In a large mixing bowl, combine pepperoni, Monterey jack cheese, cheddar cheese, oregano, onion powder and garlic powder. Mix well.
3. Brush beaten eggs over the top of wontons. Scoop equal amounts of pepperoni and cheese mixture in center of wontons. Fold sides up and over and roll wonton wrappers to form a large stick.
4. Fry sticks for about 4-5 minutes until golden brown and crispy. Remove from oil and pat dry.
5. Serve with chilled tomato dipping sauce.

Chilled tomato dipping sauce
1/4 cup tomato juice
1 cup sour cream
1 tablespoon garlic powder
1 tablespoon finely chopped fresh basil leaves
1 teaspoon dried oregano
2 pinch's pepper
1 pinch salt

Method:
1. In a small mixing bowl, combine all ingredients. Mix well.
2. Refrigerate dip for about 2 hours and serve.

GOURMET MUSHROOM, SPINACH & GOAT CHEESE TURNOVERS

Serving size- 1 party platter, 12 turnovers

Ingredients:
3 tablespoons extra virgin olive oil
3/4 cup crimini mushrooms (sliced)
3/4 cup domestic mushrooms (sliced)
3/4 cup oyster mushrooms (chopped)
3/4 cup shitaki mushrooms (stems removed and sliced)
8 oz bag baby spinach leaves (chopped)
4 ozs crumbled goat cheese
2 pinch's pepper
1 pinch salt
cooking spray
2 sheets thawed puff pastry (each sheet cut into 6 equal squares)
3 large eggs (beaten)

Method:
1. Preheat oven 375°F.
2. Drizzle olive oil in a large skillet over medium heat.
3. Sauté mushrooms for about 5 minutes stirring occasionally, add spinach and goat cheese and continue cooking and stirring until goat cheese is well blended into mushroom and spinach mixture. Season with pepper and salt. Remove from heat and cool.
4. Scoop equal amounts of mushroom mixture in center of puff pastry squares. Fold one corner of pastry to the other corner to form a triangle. Press down firmly on edges of pastry with a fork to form design.
5. Place turnovers on a sprayed baking sheet and brush with beaten eggs. Bake for about 35-40 minutes until golden brown.
6. Serve.

CRISPY MUSHROOM WONTONS

Serving size- 1 party platter, 15 wontons

Ingredients:
oil for frying
2 tablespoons extra virgin olive oil
1 large finely diced white onion
1 cup sliced domestic mushrooms
1/2 cup sliced shitaki mushrooms (stems removed)
2 tablespoons sesame oil
3 ozs cream cheese (softened)
1 tablespoon finely chopped fresh parsley
1/4 teaspoon pepper
1/4 teaspoon salt
15 wonton wrappers
3 large eggs (beaten)

Method:
1. Pour oil in a large stockpot until 1/2 full and heat to 370°F.
2. Drizzle olive oil in a large skillet over medium heat.
3. Sauté onions for about 2 minutes stirring occasionally, add mushrooms and continue cooking and stirring for about 4 minutes. Remove from heat and cool.
4. In a food processor, place mushroom mixture, sesame oil, cream cheese, parsley, pepper and salt. Blend well.
5. Brush beaten eggs over the top of the wontons, scoop equal amounts of mushroom mixture in center of wontons, fold one corner of wonton to the other corner to form a triangle. Press down firmly on edges of wonton.
6. Fry wontons for about 4-5 minutes until golden brown and crispy. Remove from oil and pat dry.
7. Serve.

RASPBERRY BAKED BRIE IN PASTRY

Serving size- 1 party platter

Ingredients:
1 sheet thawed puff pastry
3/4 cup raspberry preserves (store brought)
1 lb wheel of French Brie cheese
cooking spray
1 large egg (beaten)
1-pint fresh raspberries
(garnish) assorted crackers

Method:
1. Preheat oven 400°F.
2. Place raspberry preserve in the center of the puff pastry, top with wheel of Brie. Pull sides of pastry up over the Brie and make sure it is nice and tight. Flip pastry over on a sprayed baking sheet. Brush with beaten egg and bake for about 35-40 minutes until golden brown. Remove with a large spatula to a serving platter and top with raspberries.
3. Serve with crackers.

BEET, CHIVE AND GOAT CHEESE TART

Serving size- 1 large tart

Ingredients:
3 tablespoons extra virgin olive oil
1 1/2 lbs fresh beets (peeled and sliced)
1 small finely diced red onion
2 tablespoons finely chopped fresh chives
1 sheet thawed puff pastry
cooking spray
3 ozs crumbled goat cheese

Method:
1. Preheat oven to 375°F.
2. Drizzle olive oil in large skillet over medium heat.
3. Sauté beets for 10 minutes stirring occasionally, add onion and chives and continue cooking and stirring for about 15 minutes until beets are fork tender. Remove from heat and cool.
4. Place puff pastry on a sprayed baking sheet. Evenly spread beets and onions over puff pastry. Top with crumbled goat cheese.
5. Bake for about 35-40 minutes until pastry rises and is golden brown.
6. Serve.

MEDITERRANEAN PESTO DIP WITH PITA BREAD CHIPS

Serving size- 1 party bowl

Ingredients:
4 large round pita bread (cut into small triangle pieces)
cooking spray
paprika
2 tablespoons finely chopped fresh basil leaves
1 tablespoon fresh chopped garlic
1/2 cup extra virgin olive oil
1/4 cup pine nuts
1/2 cup canned artichoke hearts (drained)
1/2 cup sun-dried tomatoes (softened in hot water)
12oz bag baby spinach leaves (chopped)
1 tablespoon capers
1/4 teaspoon pepper
8ozs crumbled feta cheese

Method:
1. Preheat oven to 400°F.
2. Place pita triangles on sprayed baking sheet, sprinkle pita with paprika and bake for 8-10 minutes until golden brown and crispy. Remove from oven and let cool.
3. Place all other ingredients except feta cheese in a food processor and blend until all ingredients are finely chopped.
4. In a large mixing bowl, combine mixture from food processor and crumbled feta cheese. Mix well.
5. Refrigerate dip for about 2 hours.
6. Serve with pita chips.

PINEAPPLE-COCONUT-LIME AND CHILI PEPPER CHICKEN SATE

Serving size- 1 party platter, 20 sate

Ingredients:
20 6" wooden skewers (soaked in water 24 hours)
20 chicken tenderloins
2 small finely diced chili peppers
1 cup canned cream of coconut
1/4 cup pineapple juice
1/4 cup lime juice
1/2 cup extra virgin olive oil
1/4 teaspoon pepper
1/4 teaspoon salt

Method:
1. Skewer each chicken tenderloin and place in a baking dish.
2. In a small mixing bowl, combine all other ingredients. Mix well.
3. Pour mixture over chicken skewers and refrigerate for at least 24 hours.
4. Preheat grill to a medium heat.
5. Grill tenderloins for about 5 minutes and turn over. Grill for another 5 minutes or until chicken is cooked through.
6. Serve.

SUGAR CANE SKEWERED SEA SCALLOPS

Serving size- 1 party platter, 15 scallops

Ingredients:
15 canned sugar cane sticks (2-3" sticks)
15 U-10 jumbo sea scallops (picked)
1/4 cup lime juice
1/4 cup rice wine vinegar
1/4 cup apple juice
3 tablespoons extra virgin olive oil
3/4 cup all-purpose flour
1 teaspoon pepper
1 teaspoon salt
1 teaspoon cayenne pepper

Method:
1. Place sugar cane through center of sea scallops. Place in a shallow large dish.
2. In a small mixing bowl, combine lime juice, rice wine vinegar and apple juice. Mix well. Pour over scallops and refrigerate for 24 hours.
3. Drizzle olive oil in a large skillet over medium heat.
4. Remove scallops from liquid and pat dry.
5. In a large mixing bowl, combine flour, pepper, salt and cayenne pepper. Mix well.
6. Coat each scallop with flour mixture. Remove excess flour.
7. Sauté scallops for 4 minutes, then turn over and continue cooking for another 6 minutes.
8. Serve.

Side Dishes

BAKED MACARONI AND FIVE CHEESE CASSEROLE

Serving size- 1 party casserole

Ingredients:
2 tablespoons vegetable oil
1 pinch salt
1 lb elbow macaroni
1 1/2 cups milk
3 large eggs
1 cup shredded cheddar cheese
1/2 cup shredded Monterey jack cheese
8 slices white American cheese (chopped)
4 ozs cream cheese (softened)
1/4 cup grated romano cheese
2 tablespoons finely chopped fresh parsley
1 tablespoon Dijon mustard
1 teaspoon pepper
1 teaspoon salt
2 cups panko breadcrumbs
3/4 cups melted butter

Method:
1. Preheat oven 375°F.
2. Bring pot of water to a boil, drizzle 2 tablespoons of vegetable oil and a pinch of salt in water. Cook elbow pasta until just tender. Drain.
3. In a large mixing bowl, combine elbow macaroni and all other ingredients except breadcrumbs and melted butter. Mix well.
4. Place macaroni and cheese in a casserole dish.
5. In a mixing bowl, combine breadcrumbs and melted butter together. Spread breadcrumbs over the top of macaroni and cheese evenly.
6. Bake for about 35-40 minutes until topping is golden brown.
7. Serve.

PANFRIED SPAGHETTI SQUASH

Serving size- 1 bowl

Ingredients:
1 large spaghetti squash
cooking spray
3 tablespoons extra virgin olive oil
1 tablespoon chopped fresh garlic
2 tablespoons finely chopped fresh parsley
2 pinch's pepper
1 pinch salt

Method:
1. Preheat oven 400°F.
2. Cut squash in half, length wise
3. Place squash skin side up on a sprayed baking sheet.
4. Bake squash for about 45 minutes or until squash is tender. Remove from oven and cool.
5. With a large spoon, scrape squash out of the skin.
6. Drizzle olive oil in a large skillet over medium heat.
7. Sauté squash, garlic, parsley, pepper and salt for about 10 minutes, stirring occasionally.
8. Serve.

SAUTEED BROCCOLI RABE

Serving size- 1 bowl

Ingredients:
3 tablespoons extra virgin olive oil
3 bunches broccoli rabe (chopped)
1 teaspoon fresh chopped garlic
1/4 cup vegetable broth
1 teaspoon finely chopped fresh rosemary leaves
2 pinch's pepper
1 pinch salt

Method:
1. Drizzle olive oil in a large skillet over medium heat.
2. Sauté broccoli rabe for about 8 minutes stirring occasionally.
3. Add all other ingredients to skillet and continue cooking for 6-8 minutes until liquid is mostly absorbed.
4. Serve.

ITALIAN BAKED BEANS

Serving size- 1 large bean pot

Ingredients:
1/4 cup extra virgin olive oil
1 large finely diced white onion
2 large diced zucchini
1 teaspoon anchovy paste
1 tablespoon fresh chopped garlic
2 cups canned canellini beans (drained)
3 cups crushed tomatoes
1/4 cup tomato paste
1 tablespoon dried oregano
1 tablespoon dried garlic powder
1 tablespoon finely chopped basil leaves
1/2 teaspoon pepper
1/2 teaspoon salt

Method:
1. Drizzle extra virgin olive oil in a large stockpot over medium heat.
2. Sauté onions and zucchini for about 10 minutes stirring occasionally.
3. Add all other ingredients to stock pot and simmer on low heat for about 1 hour.
4. Serve.

PURPLE MASHED POTATOES WITH GOAT CHEESE

Serving size- 1 bowl

Ingredients:
3 lbs puruvian purple potatoes (washed and cut in half)
1/2 cup heavy cream
1/4 cup butter
4 ozs crumbled goat cheese
2 tablespoons finely chopped fresh parsley
1 tablespoon finely chopped fresh chives
1 teaspoon pepper
1 teaspoon salt

Method:
1. Place potatoes in a pot and fill with cold water, boil potatoes until fork tender and drain.
2. In a large mixing bowl mash potatoes, heavy cream, butter, goat cheese, parsley, chives, pepper and salt. Mix until smooth and creamy.
3. Serve.

MUSHROOM STROGANOFF

Serving size- 1 bowl

Ingredients:
2 tablespoons vegetable oil
1 pinch salt
1 lb dried linguini pasta
3 tablespoons extra virgin olive oil
1 large finely diced white onion
2 cups domestic mushrooms (sliced)
1 cup shitaki mushrooms (stems removed and sliced)
1 cup heavy cream
3/4 cup sour cream
1/4 cup worcestershire sauce
2 tablespoons finely chopped fresh parsley
1/2 teaspoon pepper
1/2 teaspoon salt

Method:
1. Bring pot of water to a boil. Drizzle 2 tablespoons vegetable oil and a pinch of salt in water. Cook linguini until just tender. Drain.
2. Drizzle olive oil in a large skillet over medium heat.
3. Sauté onions for about 2 minutes stirring occasionally. Add mushrooms and continue cooking and stirring another 5 minutes.
4. Add all other ingredients one at a time. Mix well. Add linguini and simmer on low for about 5-6 minutes.
5. Serve.

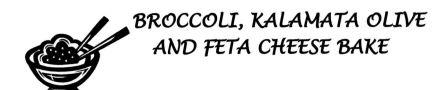
BROCCOLI, KALAMATA OLIVE AND FETA CHEESE BAKE

Serving size- 1 casserole

Ingredients:
3 large bunches broccoli (cut into florets)
2 cups canned kalamata olives (pitted)
1/4 cup extra virgin olive oil
1 tablespoon finely chopped fresh parsley
8 oz crumbled feta cheese
1 teaspoon pepper

Method:
1. Preheat oven to 350°F
2. Bring pot of water to a boil. Boil broccoli florets until just fork tender and have a nice green color to them. Drain.
3. In a large mixing bowl, combine broccoli, olives, olive oil, parsley, feta cheese and pepper. Mix well.
4. Place broccoli mix in a casserole dish.
5. Bake casserole for 10 minutes.
6. Serve.

MASHED CAULIFLOWER CASSEROLE

Serving size- 1 bowl

Ingredients:
2 heads cauliflower (cut into florets)
1/2 cup heavy cream
2 tablespoons butter
1/4 cup fresh chopped scallions
1/2 teaspoon pepper
1/2 teaspoon salt
1 cup shredded cheddar cheese

Method:
1. Preheat oven 350°F.
2. Bring pot of water to a boil. Boil cauliflower florets until fork tender. Drain.
3. In a large mixing bowl, mash cauliflower, heavy cream, butter, scallions, pepper and salt.
4. Place cauliflower mash in a casserole dish and top with cheddar cheese.
5. Bake casserole for about 15-20 minutes until cheese is melted and golden brown.
6. Serve.

CALCANNON

Serving size- 1 bowl

Ingredients:
3 lbs Yukon gold potatoes (washed, peeled and quartered)
2 tablespoons extra virgin olive oil
1 head savoy cabbage (shredded)
1/2 cup butter
3/4 cup 1/2 & 1/2
1 tablespoon finely chopped fresh thyme leaves
2 tablespoons finely chopped fresh parsley
1 teaspoon pepper
1 teaspoon salt

Method:
1. Place potatoes in a pot and fill with cold water. Boil potatoes until fork tender. Drain.
2. Drizzle olive oil in a large skillet over medium heat.
3. Sauté cabbage for about 5 minutes stirring occasionally. Remove from heat.
4. In a large mixing bowl, mash potatoes, cabbage, butter, 1/2 & 1/2, thyme, parsley, pepper and salt. Mash until smooth and creamy.
5. Serve.

TORTELLINI CARBONARA

Serving size- 1 party casserole

Ingredients:
3 small bags frozen cheese tortellini
2 tablespoons extra virgin olive oil
1 cup chopped fresh bacon
1 large finely diced white onion
1 tablespoon fresh chopped garlic
1 cup frozen sweet peas
1 1/2 cups heavy cream
1/2 cup shredded parmesan cheese
1/2 cup grated romano cheese
1 teaspoon pepper
1 teaspoon salt
1 cup shredded cheddar cheese

Method:
1. Preheat oven 350°F.
2. Bring pot of water to a boil. Cook tortellini until fork tender. Drain and cool.
3. Drizzle olive oil in a large skillet over medium heat.
4. Sauté bacon and onion for about 8-10 minutes stirring occasionally until bacon starts to get crispy. Add all other ingredients to skillet except cheddar cheese. Add tortellini to skillet and simmer on low heat for about 10 minutes.
5. Place tortellini carbonara in a casserole dish and top with cheddar cheese.
6. Bake casserole for about 15-20 minutes until cheese is melted and golden brown.
7. Serve.

MARINATED MUSHROOMS

Serving size- 1 party bowl

Ingredients:
3 cups domestic mushrooms (cut in half)
3/4 cup rice wine vinegar
3/4 cup extra virgin olive oil
1 teaspoon dried oregano
1/2 teaspoon granulated sugar
1 teaspoon lime juice
1 pinch crushed red pepper flakes
1 tablespoon fresh chopped garlic
1 pinch pepper
1 pinch salt

Method:
1. In a large mixing bowl, combine all ingredients one at a time. Mix well.
2. Refrigerate mushrooms for about 48 hours to absorb all the flavors.
3. Serve.

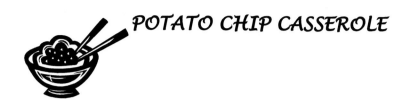

POTATO CHIP CASSEROLE

Serving size- 1 party casserole

Ingredients:
3 lbs red bliss potatoes (washed and quartered)
3/4 cup heavy cream
1/2 cup butter
1/2 cup finely chopped fresh chives
1/2 cup sour cream
1 teaspoon paprika
1 teaspoon onion powder
1 teaspoon garlic powder
1 cup shredded cheddar cheese
1 teaspoon pepper
1 teaspoon salt
1 big bag sour cream and onion potato chips (crushed)

Method:
1. Preheat oven 350°F.
2. Place potatoes in a pot and fill with cold water. Boil potatoes until fork tender. Drain.
3. In a large mixing bowl, mash potatoes and all other ingredients except potato chips. Mash until smooth and creamy.
4. Place mashed potatoes in a casserole dish and top with crushed potato chips.
5. Bake casserole for about 15-20 minutes.
6. Serve.

BUTTERED LEEK AND YUKON MASH

Serving size- 1 party bowl

Ingredients:
3 lbs Yukon gold potatoes (washed, peeled and quartered)
2 tablespoons extra virgin olive oil
1 cup diced leeks (washed and patted dry)
1/2 cup butter
3/4 cup heavy cream
1 tablespoon finely chopped fresh thymes leaves
1 teaspoon pepper
1 teaspoon salt

Method:
1. Place potatoes in a pot and fill with cold water. Boil potatoes until fork tender. Drain.
2. Drizzle olive oil in a large skillet over medium heat.
3. Sauté leeks for about 5 minutes stirring occasionally. Remove from heat.
4. In a large mixing bowl, mash potatoes, leeks, butter, heavy cream, thyme, pepper and salt. Mash well.
5. Serve.

VODKA PENNE

Serving size- 1 party casserole

Ingredients:
2 tablespoons vegetable oil
1 pinch salt
1 lb dried penna pasta
3 tablespoons extra virgin olive oil
2 pints cherry tomatoes
1 large finely diced red onion
1/4 cup vodka
2 cups heavy cream
2 tablespoons finely chopped fresh basil leaves
1/2 cup tomato paste
1 pinch crushed red pepper flakes
1/2 cup shredded parmesan cheese
1/2 cup grated romano cheese
1 teaspoon pepper
1 teaspoon salt
1 cup shredded mozzarella cheese

Method:
1. Preheat oven 350°F.
2. Bring pot of water to a boil, drizzle 2 tablespoons vegetable oil and a pinch of salt in water. Cook penne until just tender. Drain.
3. Drizzle olive oil in a large skillet over medium heat.
4. Sauté tomatoes and onion for 5 minutes stirring occasionally.
5. Remove skillet from heat and add vodka. Return skillet to heat and cook for 2-3 minutes.
6. Add heavy cream, basil, tomato paste, crushed red pepper, parmesan cheese, romano cheese, pepper and salt to skillet. Add penna pasta and simmer on low for about 10 minutes.
7. Place pasta in a casserole dish and cover with mozzarella cheese.
8. Bake casserole for about 15-20 minutes until cheese is melted and golden brown.
9. Serve.

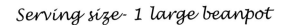 # CHIPOTLE BBQ BAKED BEANS

Serving size- 1 large beanpot

Ingredients:
1/4 cup extra virgin olive oil
1 cup chopped fresh bacon
1 large finely diced white onion
2 cups canned small red beans
1 bottle lite beer
1 cup ketchup
1 cup canned crushed tomatoes
1/4 cup molasses
2 tablespoons granulated sugar
1/4 cup finely chopped canned chipotle peppers
2 tablespoons finely chopped fresh parsley
1 tablespoon dark chili powder
2 tablespoons finely chopped fresh cilantro leaves
1 teaspoon pepper
1 teaspoon salt

Method:
1. Drizzle olive oil in a large stockpot over medium heat.
2. Sauté bacon and onions for about 10 minutes stirring occasionally.
3. Add beans and beer. Cook and stir for another 10 minutes.
4. Add all other ingredients one at a time. Stir well.
5. Simmer beans on a low heat for about 1 hour.
6. Serve.

SAVORY HERB BREAD PUDDING LOAF

Serving size- 1 large loaf

Ingredients:
Cooking spray
20 slices white sandwich bread (crust removed and diced)
1 tablespoon fresh chopped garlic
1 tablespoon finely chopped fresh parsley
1 tablespoon finely chopped fresh rosemary leaves
1 tablespoon finely chopped fresh thyme leaves
1 tablespoon finely chopped fresh oregano leaves
1 tablespoon finely chopped fresh sage leaves
1 small finely diced red onion
1 1/2 cups heavy cream
6 large eggs
1 teaspoon pepper
1 teaspoon salt

Method:
1. Preheat oven 375°F.
2. Spray loaf pan with cooking spray.
3. In a large mixing bowl, combine all ingredients, Mix well.
4. Place bread mixture in a sprayed loaf pan.
5. Bake loaf for about 40-45 minutes.
6. Remove from oven and cool for about 10 minutes.
7. Turn loaf pan over a plate and remove bread pudding loaf.
8. Slice and serve.

BEER BATTERED ASPARAGUS SPEARS
(with a creole mustard sauce)

Serving size- 1 party platter, 20 asparagus spears

Ingredients:
20 large asparagus spears
ice water
oil for frying
2 bottles lite beer
1 cup unbleached flour
2 large eggs
1/2 teaspoon pepper
1/2 teaspoon salt
1 cup all-purpose flour

Method:
1. Bring pot of water to a boil.
2. Cut off 1 1/2 to 2" from the bottom of each asparagus spear. Cook spears in water for about 5 minutes, make sure they have a nice green color to them. Remove from the hot water and place in ice water.
3. Cool for about 10 minutes. Remove from ice water and pat dry.
4. Pour oil in a large stockpot until 1/2 full and heat to 370°F.
5. In a large mixing bowl, combine all other ingredients except the all-purpose flour. Mix well.
6. Lightly coat the asparagus spears in all-purpose flour and then dip asparagus into batter.
7. Fry asparagus spears for about 3-4 minutes until crispy and golden brown.
8. Serve with creole mustard sauce.

CREOLE MUSTARD SAUCE

Ingredients:
1 tablespoon whole grain mustard
1/2 teaspoon cayenne pepper
1 cup sour cream
1 tablespoon finely chopped fresh parsley
2 pinch's pepper
1 pinch salt

Method:
1. In a small mixing bowl, combine all ingredients. Mix well.
2. Refrigerate sauce for about 1 hour.
3. Serve.

PRETZEL CRUSTED MASHED POTATO PANCAKES

Serving size- 1 party platter-15 cakes

Ingredients:
3 lbs red bliss potatoes (washed and quartered)
1/4 cup extra virgin olive oil
1/4 cup Dijon mustard
1/4 cup finely chopped fresh chives
1/4 cup prepared horseradish
1/2 cup sour cream
1 teaspoon pepper
1 teaspoon salt
2 cups all-purpose flour
6 large eggs
2 cups 1/2 & 1/2
2 cups ground pretzels (unsalted)
1/2 cup unseasoned breadcrumbs
(garnish) sour cream

Method:
1. Preheat oven 350°F.
2. Place potatoes in a pot and fill with cold water. Boil potatoes until fork tender. Drain and cool.
3. Drizzle olive oil in a large skillet over medium heat.
4. In a large mixing bowl, mash potatoes, mustard, chives, horseradish, sour cream, pepper, salt and all-purpose flour. Mix well.
5. Divide potato mixture into 12 equal portions and form into cakes.
6. In a small mixing bowl, beat eggs and 1/2 & 1/2. Mix well.
7. In another small mixing bowl, combine ground pretzels and breadcrumbs.
8. Dip each cake in egg mixture and coat in pretzel mixture.
9. Sauté cakes for about 4 minutes, turn cakes over and place skillet in oven for about 15 minutes.
10. Serve with sour cream.

IRISH POTATO CROQUETS

Serving size - 1 party platter

Ingredients:
2 lbs red bliss potatoes (washed & quartered)
oil for frying
1/2 cup all purpose flour
2 large eggs
3/4 cup chopped cooked bacon
1/4 cup finely chopped fresh chives
1 teaspoon pepper
1/2 teaspoon salt
3/4 cup unbleached flour
3 large eggs
1 cup 1/2 & 1/2
2 cups unseasoned breadcrumbs
(garnish) sour cream

Method:
1. Place potatoes in a pot and fill with cold water. Boil potatoes until fork tender. Drain and cool.
2. Pour oil in a large stockpot until 1/2 full and heat to 370°F.
3. In a large mixing bowl, mash potatoes, all purpose flour, eggs, bacon, chives, pepper and salt. Mix well.
4. Form golf ball size croquets with equal amounts of potato mixture.
5. Coat potatoes in unbleached flour.
6. In a small mixing bowl, beat eggs and cream together. Mix well.
7. One at a time, dip the croquets in egg mixture and then in breadcrumbs.
8. Fry croquets for about 5 minutes, remove from oil and pat dry.
9. Serve with sour cream.

SPICY JALAPENO CORN CAKES

Serving size- 1 party platter, 20 cakes

Ingredients:
1/4 cup extra virgin olive oil
3 cups canned whole kernel corn (drained)
2 small finely diced jalapeño peppers
1 small finely diced red bell pepper
1 small finely diced green bell pepper
1 small finely diced white onion
1 cup unbleached flour
1/2 teaspoon crushed red pepper flakes
2 tablespoons finely chopped fresh cilantro leaves
5 large eggs
1 teaspoon pepper
1 teaspoon salt
1 cup all purpose flour
(garnish) sour cream

Method:
1. Preheat oven 350°F.
2. Drizzle olive oil in a large skillet over medium heat.
3. In a large mixing bowl, combine all ingredients except all-purpose flour, one at a time. Mix well.
4. Divide mixture into 20 equal portions and form into cakes.
5. Lightly coat cakes with all-purpose flour.
6. Sauté cakes for about 5 minutes. Turn cakes over and place skillet in oven for about 15 minutes.
7. Serve with sour cream.

JAMAICAN JERK ROASTED POTATOES

Serving size - 1 party platter

Ingredients:
3 lbs all purpose potatoes (washed, peeled & quartered)
1/2 cup extra virgin olive oil
1 small finely diced red onion
1 small finely diced red bell pepper
1 small finely diced green bell pepper
1 tablespoon dried thyme
1 tablespoon garlic powder
1 teaspoon cayenne pepper
1 tablespoon onion powder
1 teaspoon all spice
1 teaspoon cayenne pepper
1 pinch crushed red pepper flakes
1 teaspoon pepper
1 teaspoon salt

Method:
1. Preheat oven 375°F.
2. In a large mixing bowl, combine all ingredients. Mix well.
3. Place potatoes on a baking sheet and roast for about 1 hour to 1 hour and 15 minutes until potatoes are golden brown and fork tender.
4. Serve.

PESTO AND CRUMBLED BLUE CHEESE STUFFED TOMATOES

Serving size- 1 party casserole, 10 stuffed tomatoes

Ingredients:
10 large vine ripened red tomatoes
1 large bunch fresh basil leaves (washed and patted dry)
1/2 cup extra virgin olive oil
1/2 cup shredded parmesan cheese
1 tablespoon fresh chopped garlic
1/4 cup pine nuts
1/2 teaspoon pepper
1/2 teaspoon salt
1 cup unseasoned breadcrumbs
1 cup crumbled blue cheese
1/2 cup melted butter

Method:
1. Preheat oven 350°F.
2. Remove top and inside of all 10 tomatoes.
3. In a food processor, puree basil leaves, olive oil, parmesan cheese, garlic, pine nuts, pepper and salt to make the pesto.
4. In a large mixing bowl, combine pesto, breadcrumbs, blue cheese and butter. Mix well.
5. Stuff tomatoes with mixture and place side by side in a casserole dish.
6. Bake casserole for about 30-35 minutes.
7. Serve.

DRUNKEN ONIONS

Servings size- 1 bowl

Ingredients:
3 lbs fresh pearl onions (peeled)
1/4 cup sherry wine
1/4 cup whiskey
2 tablespoons finely chopped fresh parsley
1 tablespoon fresh chopped garlic
1 teaspoon pepper
1 teaspoon salt
3 tablespoons extra virgin olive oil

Method:
1. Place all ingredients except olive oil in a large zip lock bag and shake well.
2. Refrigerate zip lock bag for about 24 hours.
3. Drizzle olive oil in a large skillet over medium heat.
4. Drain onions.
5. Sauté onions for about 15 minutes stirring occasionally until onions are nice and tender.
6. Serve.

Sandwiches, Burgers, Pizzas and Calzones

 # SLOPPY B'S

Serving size- 1 party platter, 8 large sandwiches

Ingredients:
2 tablespoons extra virgin olive oil
2 lbs ground beef (85% lean)
1 small finely diced white onion
1 teaspoon onion powder
1 teaspoon dark chili powder
1 tablespoon Worcestershire sauce
2 tablespoons tomato paste
1/2 cup ketchup
2 tablespoons molasses
1 tablespoon brown sugar
1 teaspoon pepper
1 teaspoon salt
8 large potato bread rolls (split)
1 cup shredded cheddar cheese

Method:
1. Drizzle olive oil in a large skillet over medium heat.
2. Sauté ground beef and onions for about 15 minutes stirring occasionally.
3. Add onion powder, chili powder, Worcestershire sauce, tomato paste, ketchup, molasses, brown sugar, pepper and salt.
4. Simmer over low heat for about 10 minutes.
5. Place equal amounts of ground beef mixture over the bottom of each roll. Top with shredded cheddar cheese and top of roll.
6. Serve.

ITALIAN MUFFALETTA

Serving size- 1 large sandwich

Ingredients:
1 large oval Italian bread loaf cut in half, length ways (inside removed)
1 lb sliced ham deli meat
1/2 lb sliced mortadella deli meat
1/2 lb sliced cappicola deli meat
1/2 lb sliced salami deli meat
1 lb sliced pepperoni
1/2 lb sliced mozzarella cheese
1/2 lb sliced provolone cheese
1/2 head iceberg lettuce (shredded)
1 cup finely diced plum tomatoes
1 large thinly sliced red onion
1 cup canned pepperoncini's (chopped)
1/2 cup Italian dressing (store bought)

Method:
1. Preheat oven 325°F.
2. Layer slices of meat inside bottom of bread loaf. Layer sliced cheese on top meat and cover with top of bread loaf.
3. Place bread loaf on a baking sheet and bake for about 8-10 minutes. Remove from oven and let cool.
4. In a large mixing bowl, combine all other ingredients, Mix well.
5. Remove the top of the loaf. Place lettuce mixture on top of meats and cheese and cover with the top of bread loaf.
6. Serve.

GRILLED ROAST BEEF SANDWICHES

Serving size- 1 party platter, 6 sandwiches

Ingredients:
2 tablespoons butter
12 slices thick sour dough bread
1 lb sliced rare roast beef deli meat
12 slices muenster cheese
12 slices vine ripened red tomatoes
1 tablespoon prepared horseradish
1/2 cup mayonnaise
2 pinch's pepper
1 pinch salt

Method:
1. In a large skillet over medium heat, melt butter.
2. Equally portion roast beef on top of 6 slices of bread. Top roast beef with muenster cheese and tomatoes.
3. In a small mixing bowl, combine horseradish, mayonnaise, pepper and salt. Mix well. Spread mayonnaise mixture evenly over 6 remaining slices of bread. Place on top of tomatoes, mayonnaise side down.
4. Place sandwiches in skillet for about 4-5 minutes until golden brown, Flip sandwiches over and cook for another 4 minutes.
5. Serve.

TOASTED TURKEY CORDON BLEU SANDWICHES

Serving size- 1 party platter, 8 sandwiches

Ingredients:
8 large round Kaiser rolls (split)
1 lb sliced roasted turkey deli meat
1 lb sliced ham deli meat
1/2 lb sliced swiss cheese
1/2 cup mayonnaise
1 teaspoon finely chopped fresh thyme leaves
2 pinch's pepper
1 pinch salt

Method:
1. Preheat oven 325°F.
2. On the bottom part of the Kaiser rolls, top with equal portions of turkey, ham and swiss cheese.
3. In a small mixing bowl, combine mayonnaise, fresh thyme, pepper and salt. Mix well.
4. Spread mayonnaise mixture evenly over the meats and cheese. Cover with kaiser roll top.
5. Place sandwiches on baking sheet and bake for about 5-8 minutes until rolls are nice and toasted.
6. Serve.

BUFFALO TURKEY WRAP

Serving size- 1 party platter, 8 wraps

Ingredients:
8 12" flour tortillas
3/4 cup Barry's favorite blue cheese dressing
1/2 head green cabbage (shredded)
1 cup finely diced plum tomatoes
2 lbs sliced roasted turkey deli meat
1/4 cup buffalo hot sauce
4 ozs crumbled blue cheese

Method:
1. In a large mixing bowl, combine blue cheese dressing, cabbage and plum tomatoes. Mix well.
2. Spread equal amounts of cabbage mixture over the top of the tortillas
3. In a small mixing bowl, combine sliced turkey and hot sauce. Coat well.
4. Place equal amount of turkey over cabbage mixture and top with crumbled blue cheese.
5. Fold sided of tortillas up and over, and roll tortillas tight.
6. Serve.

MINI LAMB AND GOAT CHEESE BURGERS
(With a garlic rosemary mayonnaise)

Serving size- 1 party platter, 12 mini burgers

Ingredients:
2 lbs fresh ground lamb
4 ozs crumbled goat cheese
2 pinch's pepper
1 pinch salt
2 tablespoons extra virgin olive oil
1 teaspoon finely chopped fresh rosemary leaves
1 teaspoon fresh chopped garlic
1 small finely diced red onion
1/2 cup mayonnaise
12 2" round mini burger rolls (split)

Method:
1. In a large mixing bowl, combine ground lamb, goat cheese, pepper and salt. Mix well.
2. Divide lamb mixture into 12 equal portions and form patties.
3. Drizzle olive oil in a large skillet over medium heat.
4. Cook burgers in skillet for about 5 minutes, flip burgers over and cook for another 5 minutes. Remove from heat.
5. In a small mixing bowl, combine rosemary, garlic, red onion and mayonnaise. Mix well.
6. Spread mayonnaise mixture on the inside of the bottom burger roll and top with a pattie. Cover with tops.
7. Serve.

SURF AND TURF BURGER

Serving size- 1 party platter, 6 burgers

Ingredients:
2 lbs fresh ground sirloin
1 tablespoon fresh chopped garlic
2 tablespoons extra virgin olive oil
1 cup fresh cooked lobster meat (chopped)
1/4 cup mayonnaise
1 teaspoon finely chopped fresh tarragon leaves
1 teaspoon lemon juice
2 pinch's pepper
1 pinch salt
5 large sesame rolls (split)

Method:
1. In a large mixing bowl, combine ground sirloin and garlic. Mix well.
2. Divide sirloin mixture into 6 equal portions. Form into patties.
3. Drizzle olive oil in a large skillet over medium heat.
4. Cook burgers for about 8 minutes, flip burgers over and cook for another 8 minutes. Remove from heat.
5. In a small mixing bowl, combine lobster, mayonnaise, tarragon, lemon juice, pepper and salt. Mix well.
6. Place patties on the bottom of the rolls, top burgers with equal portions of lobster salad. Cover with roll tops.
7. Serve.

VEAL PARMESAN BURGER

Serving size- 1 party platter, 6 burgers

Ingredients:
2 lbs ground veal
1 tablespoon dried oregano
1 tablespoon garlic powder
2 tablespoons grated romano cheese
1/2 teaspoon pepper
1/2 teaspoon salt
1 tablespoons extra virgin olive oil
3/4 cup finely diced plum tomatoes
1 tablespoon finely chopped fresh basil leaves
1 tablespoon fresh chopped garlic
6 slices provolone cheese
6 square foccacia rolls (split)

Method:
1. Preheat oven 350°F.
2. In a large mixing bowl, combine ground veal, oregano, garlic powder, romano cheese, pepper and salt. Mix well.
3. Divide veal mixture into 6 equal portions. Form into patties.
4. Drizzle olive oil in a large skillet over medium heat.
5. Cook burgers for about 8 minutes, flip burgers and cook for another 8 minutes. Remove from heat.
6. In a small mixing bowl, combine tomatoes, basil and garlic. Mix well.
7. Place patties on bottom of foccacia rolls, top with equal portions of tomato mixture and provolone cheese. Cover with foccacia roll top.
8. Place burgers on a baking sheet and bake for about 5-6 minutes until roll is nice and toasted.
9. Serve.

 # BASIC PIZZA DOUGH

Serving size- 1 batch dough

Ingredients:
1/4 oz (1 package) active dry yeast
1 cup warm water
3 cups unbleached flour
1 teaspoon salt
1 pinch sugar
vegetable oil

Method:
1. In a large mixing bowl, dissolve yeast in warm water for about 5 minutes.
2. With the mixer on low speed, add flour a little at a time until all is incorporated, add salt and sugar. Turn mixer to high speed and mix for 2 minutes. Remove dough from bowl and knead by hand on a lightly floured surface.
3. Form dough into a ball and place in the center of an oiled bowl and cover with plastic wrap. Place in a warm area for about 1 hour until dough doubles in size.
4. Punch down dough and let stand for 2 minutes.
5. Ready to use.

PIZZA PUTTANESCA

Serving size- 1 large pizza

Ingredients:
1 batch basic pizza dough
cooking spray
1/4 cup extra virgin olive oil
1 small finely diced red onion
1/2 cup canned crushed tomatoes
1 tablespoon capers
1 tablespoon anchovy paste
1 tablespoon canned tomato paste
1/2 cup canned black olives (pitted, sliced & drained)
1 tablespoon finely chopped fresh oregano leaves
1 tablespoon finely chopped fresh basil leaves
1 teaspoon fresh chopped garlic
2 tablespoons grated romano cheese
1 cup shredded mozzarella cheese
1 cup shredded cheddar cheese

Method:
1. Preheat oven 350°F.
2. On a sprayed 16" pizza pan, press dough to form crust. Set aside.
3. In a large mixing bowl, combine olive oil, red onion, crushed tomatoes, capers, anchovy paste, tomato paste, olives, oregano, basil, garlic and romano. Mix well.
4. Spread mixture evenly over pizza dough. Top with mozzarella and cheddar cheese.
5. Bake pizza for 35-40 minutes until golden brown.
6. Serve.

MUSHROOM POMADORO PIZZA

Serving size- 1 large pizza

Ingredients:
1 batch basic pizza dough
cooking spray
2 cups finely diced plum tomatoes
1/4 cup extra virgin olive oil
2 tablespoons finely chopped fresh basil leaves
2 pinch's pepper
1 pinch salt
1 cup shredded mozzarella cheese
1 cup shredded fontina cheese
1 cup sliced crimini mushrooms

Method:
1. Preheat oven 350°F.
2. In a sprayed 16" pizza pan, press dough to form crust. Set aside.
3. In a large mixing bowl, combine tomatoes, olive oil, basil, pepper and salt. Mix well.
4. Spread tomato mixture evenly over pizza dough, top with mozzarella, fontina cheese and mushrooms.
5. Bake pizza for 35-40 minutes until golden brown.
6. Serve.

 # PIZZA FLORENTINE

Serving size- 1 large pizza

Ingredients:
1 batch basic pizza dough
cooking spray
1/4 cup extra virgin olive oil
8 oz bag baby spinach leaves (chopped)
2 pinch's pepper
1 cup shredded cheddar cheese
1/2 cup shredded Monterey jack cheese
4 ozs crumbled feta cheese

Method:
1. Preheat oven 350°F.
2. On a sprayed 16" pizza pan, press dough to form crust. Set aside.
3. In a large mixing bowl, combine olive oil, spinach and pepper. Mix well.
4. Spread spinach mixture evenly over pizza dough, top with cheddar, Monterey jack and feta cheese.
5. Bake pizza for 35-40 minutes until golden brown.
6. Serve.

SPICY SAUSAGE CALZONE

Serving size- 1 large calzone

Ingredients:
2 tablespoons extra virgin olive oil
8 hot Italian sausages (casing removed)
1 small finely diced white onion
1 large finely diced red bell pepper
1 large finely diced green bell pepper
1 tablespoon fresh chopped garlic
2 tablespoons dried oregano
1 batch basic pizza dough
cooking spray
2 cups shredded mozzarella cheese
1 large egg (beaten)

Method:
1. Preheat oven 350°F.
2. Drizzle olive oil in a large skillet over medium heat.
3. Sauté sausage, onion and pepper for about 10-12 minutes, stirring occasionally. Stir in garlic and oregano. Remove from heat.
4. Stretch pizza dough to a 16" circle.
5. Spray baking sheet. Set aside.
6. Spread sausage mixture in center of dough, top with mozzarella cheese. Fold dough over and press edges together. Place calzone on sprayed baking sheet, Brush with beaten egg.
7. Bake calzone for about 35-40 minutes until brown.
8. Serve.

LOBSTER & SPINACH CALZONE

Serving size- 1 large calzone

Ingredients:
1 batch basic pizza dough
cooking spray
2 cups ricotta cheese
1 cup fresh cooked lobster meat (chopped)
1 8oz bag baby spinach leaves (chopped)
1/4 cup grated romano cheese
1 tablespoon garlic powder
1 tablespoon dried oregano
1 large egg (beaten)

Method:
1. Preheat oven 350°F.
2. Spray baking sheet. Set aside.
3. Stretch pizza dough to a 16" circle.
4. In a large mixing bowl, combine all other ingredients except beaten egg. Mix well.
5. Spread mixture in the center of dough, fold dough over and press edges together. Place calzone on sprayed baking sheet. Brush with beaten egg.
6. Bake calzone for 35-40 minutes until golden brown.
7. Serve.

Seafood

SKILLET MUSSELS

Serving size- 1 party bowl

Ingredients:
3 tablespoons extra virgin olive oil
1 large finely diced red onion
1 large finely diced red bell pepper
1 large finely diced green bell pepper
3 lbs Prince Edward Island mussels
1/2 cup white wine
1 tablespoon finely chopped fresh basil leaves
2 tablespoons lemon juice
1/4 cup canned tomato paste
1/2 cup heavy cream
2 tablespoons butter
1/2 teaspoon pepper
1/2 teaspoon salt

Method:
1. Drizzle olive oil in a large skillet over medium-high heat.
2. Sauté onions and peppers for about 5 minutes stirring occasionally. Add mussels and white wine and cover for about 3-5 minutes until mussel shells start to open. Remove cover and add all other ingredients. Mix well.
3. Lower heat to a simmer and continue cooking for about 4 minutes.
4. Serve.

BAKED HALIBUT PARMESAN

Serving size- 1 party platter, 6 fish filets

Ingredients:
6 (8oz) halibut filets (skinless & boneless)
3/4 cup Italian seasoned breadcrumbs
1/4 cup grated parmesan cheese
1/4 cup extra virgin olive oil
1 cup finely diced plum tomatoes
1 teaspoon dried oregano
1 teaspoon fresh chopped garlic
1 teaspoon finely chopped fresh basil leaves
6 slices mozzarella cheese

Method:
1. Preheat oven 375°F.
2. In a small mixing bowl, combine seasoned breadcrumbs and parmesan cheese. Mix well.
3. Coat each halibut filet in breadcrumbs. Coat well. Place each filet on a baking sheet.
4. Drizzle filets with olive oil and bake for about 20-25 minutes.
5. In a small mixing bowl, combine tomatoes, oregano, garlic and basil. Mix well.
6. Remove halibut from oven and top with equal amounts of tomato mixture.
7. Place one slice of mozzarella cheese on top of tomato mixture. Place baking sheet back in the oven and bake for another 5 minutes until cheese is melted.
8. Serve.

TAVERN SWORDFISH
(With a dijon scallion butter)

Serving size- 1 party platter, 6 swordfish steaks

Ingredients:
1/4 cup extra virgin olive oil
6 (8oz) swordfish steaks
1 cup ground pretzels (unsalted)
1/2 cup unseasoned breadcrumbs
1/2 cup butter
2 tablespoons dijon mustard
2 tablespoons fresh chopped scallions
2 pinch's pepper
1 pinch salt
lemon wedges (garnish)

Method:
1. Drizzle olive oil in a large skillet over medium heat.
2. In a large mixing bowl, combine ground pretzels and breadcrumbs. Mix well.
3. Coat swordfish steaks in breadcrumb mixture.
4. Cook swordfish steaks in skillet for 6-8 minutes. Turn steaks over and continue cooking for 6-8 more minutes until nice and golden brown. Remove swordfish steaks from skillet and place on a platter. Add all other ingredients to skillet. Stir until melted. Drizzle over swordfish.
6. Garnish with lemon wedges and serve.

ENGLISHMAN'S FRIED HADDOCK

Serving size- 1 party basket

Ingredients:
oil for frying
2 lbs haddock fillets (skinless, boneless & cut into 2-3" pieces)
1 cup unbleached flour
1/2 teaspoon pepper
1/2 teaspoon salt
1 tablespoon paprika
4 large eggs
1 cup 1/2 & 1/2
(garnish) malt vinegar
(garnish) tartar sauce
(garnish) lemon wedges

Method:
1. Pour oil in a large stockpot until 1/2 full and heat to 370°F.
2. In a large mixing bowl, combine flour, pepper, salt and paprika. Mix well. Set aside.
3. In another large mixing bowl, beat eggs and 1/2 & 1/2 together.
4. Coat each piece of haddock in flour, then dip haddock in egg mixture. Repeat twice until well coated.
5. Fry haddock for about 5-6 minutes until nice and golden brown.
6. Line a basket with wax paper. Remove haddock from oil and place in basket.
7. Serve with vinegar, tartar sauce and lemon wedges.

ASIAN GRILLED TUNA STEAKS

Serving size- 1 party platter, 6 steaks

Ingredients:
6 (8oz) yellow fin tuna steaks
1/2 cup soy sauce
1/2 cup teriyaki sauce
1/2 cup sesame oil
1/2 cup extra virgin olive oil
2 tablespoons lemon juice
2 pinch's pepper
(garnish) pickled ginger (store bought)
(garnish) lemon wedges

Method:
1. In a large zip-lock bag, combine soy sauce, teriyaki, sesame oil, olive oil, lemon juice and pepper. Place tuna steaks in zip-lock bag and refrigerate for 2 hours.
2. Preheat grill to a medium heat.
3. Remove tuna steaks from marinade.
4. Grill tuna steaks for 3-4 minutes. Flip steaks over and grill another 3-4 minutes. Remove from grill.
5. Serve with pickled ginger and lemon wedges.

CARRIBEAN RED SNAPPER FILET

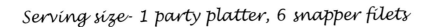

Serving size- 1 party platter, 6 snapper filets

Ingredients:
6 (8oz) red snapper filets, skin on (boneless)
3/4 cup extra virgin olive oil
1/4 cup lime juice
1 tablespoon onion powder
1 teaspoon garlic pepper
1 teaspoon cayenne pepper
1 teaspoon all-spice
1 teaspoon crushed dried thyme
1 teaspoon nutmeg
1 teaspoon pepper
1/2 teaspoon salt

Method:
1. Preheat oven 350°F.
2. In a large mixing bowl, combine olive oil, lime juice, onion powder, garlic powder, cayenne pepper, all spice, thyme, nutmeg, pepper and salt. Mix well.
3. Coat each snapper filet evenly with seasoning mixture.
4. Place snapper filets on baking sheet and bake for about 30-35 minutes. Remove from oven.
5. Serve.

LEMON, LIME AND GARLIC GRILLED SHRIMP SATE

Serving size- 1 party platter, 20 sate

Ingredients:
20 6" wooden skewers (soaked in warm water for 24 hrs)
20 U-15 black tiger shrimp (peeled and de-veined)
1 cup extra virgin olive oil
1 cup lemon juice
1/4 cup lime juice
zest from 1 lemon
zest from 1 lime
1 tablespoon fresh chopped garlic
2 pinch's pepper
1 pinch salt

Method:
1. Place skewers through center of shrimp from tail to head.
2. In a large zip-lock bag, combine olive oil, lemon juice, lime juice, lemon zest, lime zest, garlic, pepper and salt. Place skewers in zip-lock bag.
3. Refrigerate shrimp for about 24 hours.
4. Preheat grill to a medium heat.
5. Remove shrimp from marinade.
6. Grill shrimp skewers for about 3-4 minutes. Turn shrimp and cook another 3-4 minutes. Remove from grill.
7. Serve.

QUICK BAKED STUFFED LOBSTERS
(with a rock shrimp and buttered leek stuffing)

Serving size- 1 party platter, 6 lobsters

Ingredients:
6 (1 1/4 lb) lobsters (already steamed)
2 tablespoons extra virgin olive oil
2 lbs rock shrimp (peeled and cleaned)
1 cup diced leeks (washed and patted dry)
2 cups ground ritz crackers
3/4 cup butter (melted)
1/2 teaspoon pepper
1/2 teaspoon salt

Method:
1. Preheat oven 375°F.
2. With a sharp knife tip, cut a slit down the center of the lobsters belly and tail. Open lobster.
3. Place lobsters on baking sheet with bellies facing up. Set aside.
4. Drizzle olive oil in a large skillet over medium heat.
5. Sauté shrimp and leeks for about 5-6 minutes until shrimp have a nice pink color to them. Remove from heat.
6. In a large mixing bowl, combine crackers, butter, pepper, salt and shrimp mixture. Mix well.
7. Stuff the lobsters with equal amounts of stuffing mixture.
8. Bake lobster for about 20 minutes until stuffing turns a nice golden brown color.
9. Serve.

HERBED POLENTA BAKED SALMON
(with an arugala pesto cream sauce)

Serving size- 1 party platter

Ingredients:
1 (3-4 lb) side of salmon (filet) (skinless & boneless)
1 cup dried polenta
1 tablespoon finely chopped fresh parsley
1 teaspoon finely chopped fresh basil leaves
1 teaspoon finely chopped fresh dill
1/2 teaspoon pepper
1/2 teaspoon salt
cooking spray
2 tablespoons extra virgin olive oil

Method:
1. Preheat oven 375°F.
2. In a large mixing bowl, combine polenta, parsley, basil, dill, pepper and salt. Mix well.
3. Coat the whole salmon filet with polenta mixture. Coat well.
4. Place salmon on sprayed baking sheet.
5. Drizzle salmon with olive oil.
6. Bake salmon for about 30-35 minutes. Remove from oven and let cool for about 4-5 minutes. With a large spatulas, remove salmon filet from baking sheet and place on platter.
7. Serve with arugula pesto cream sauce.

Arugula Pesto Cream Sauce

Ingredients:
1 bunch fresh arugula (chopped, washed & patted dry)
1/2 cup extra virgin olive oil
3 tablespoons sour cream
1/4 cup pine nuts
2 tablespoons fresh chopped garlic
1/4 cup shredded parmesan cheese
1/4 teaspoon pepper
1/4 teaspoon salt

Method:
1. Place all ingredients in a food processor and puree until smooth & creamy.
2. Serve.

POACHED SALMON STUFFED JUMBO PASTA SHELLS

Serving size- 1 party casserole

Ingredients:
2 lbs salmon filet (skinless & boneless)
2 tablespoons vegetable oil
1 pinch salt
1 lb dried jumbo pasta shells
2 cups ricotta cheese
2 tablespoons finely chopped fresh dill
1 tablespoon onion powder
2 cups heavy cream
2 large eggs
1 cup grated romano cheese
1/2 teaspoon pepper
1/2 teaspoon salt
2 tablespoons finely chopped fresh chives
2 tablespoons finely chopped fresh parsley
1 cup shredded cheddar cheese

Method:
1. Bring pot of water to a boil. Then turn heat down to a medium. Poach salmon filet for 5 minutes.
2. Drain salmon and let cool.
3. Bring pot of water to a boil, drizzle 2 tablespoons vegetable oil and pinch of salt in water. Cook pasta shells until just tender. Drain and cool under cold water. Leave in colander to drain.
4. Preheat oven to 350°F.
5. In a large mixing bowl, combine salmon, ricotta cheese, dill and onion powder.
6. Stuff each pasta shell with equal amounts of salmon stuffing. Place shells in a casserole dish.
7. In a large mixing bowl, beat heavy cream, eggs, romano cheese, pepper, salt, chives and parsley. Pour cream mixture over the shells. Top with shredded cheddar cheese.
8. Bake casserole for about 20-25 minutes until cheese is golden brown.
9. Serve.

BAKED STUFFED SHRIMP
(with a crab stuffing)

Serving size- 1 party platter, 20 stuffed shrimp

Ingredients:
20 U-15 black tiger shrimp (peeled and de-veined. Tails left on)
1 1/2 lbs fresh lump crabmeat
6 slices white sandwich bread (crust removed and diced)
1 tablespoon ground mustard
1/2 cup mayonnaise
2 large eggs
1/2 cup panko breadcrumbs
2 tablespoons lemon juice
1/2 teaspoon pepper
1/2 teaspoon salt
1/2 cup butter (melted)

Method:
1. Preheat oven 350°F.
2. With a sharp knife, butterfly the shrimp.
3. In a large mixing bowl, combine crabmeat, diced bread, mustard, mayonnaise, eggs, breadcrumbs, lemon juice, pepper and salt. Mix well.
4. Divide crab mixture into 20 equal portions.
5. Stuff the inside of shrimp with crab mixture and pull the tail up and over.
6. Place shrimp on a baking sheet and drizzle with melted butter.
7. Bake shrimp for about 20-25 minutes.
8. Serve.

Poultry

CREAMY CHICKEN GORGONZOLA

Serving size- 1 party platter

Ingredients:
3 tablespoons extra virgin olive oil
6 (8oz) boneless skinless chicken breasts (thinly pounded and cut in half)
3/4 cup all-purpose flour
1 cup domestic mushrooms (sliced)
1/2 cup sun-dried tomatoes (softened in hot water)
8 oz bag baby spinach leaves (chopped)
1 cup heavy cream
8 oz Gorgonzola cheese
2 pinch's pepper
1 pinch salt

Method:
1. Drizzle olive oil in a large skillet over medium heat.
2. Lightly flour each piece of chicken. Remove any excess flour.
3. Place chicken breast in skillet and cook for about 5-6 minutes. Turn chicken over and add mushrooms. Cook for another 5 minutes. Add sun-dried tomatoes and spinach.
4. Add heavy cream, Gorgonzola cheese, peppers and salt, stirring frequently.
5. Reduce heat to a simmer and cook for 4-5 minutes.
6. Serve.

CHICKEN BRUSCHETTA

Serving size- 1 party platter

Ingredients:
3 tablespoons extra virgin olive oil
6 (8oz) boneless skinless chicken breasts (thinly pounded and cut in half)
3/4 cup all-purpose flour
1 pint cherry tomatoes
1 tablespoon fresh chopped garlic
1 tablespoon finely chopped fresh basil leaves
1 cup heavy cream
4 ozs crumbled goat cheese
2 pinch's pepper
1 pinch salt

Method:
1. Drizzle olive oil in a large skillet over medium heat.
2. Lightly flour each piece of chicken. Remove any excess flour.
3. Place chicken breast in skillet and cook for about 5-6 minutes. Turn chicken over and add cherry tomatoes and garlic. Cook for another 5 minutes.
4. Add all other ingredients, one at a time, stirring frequently.
5. Reduce heat to a simmer and cook for 4-5 minutes.
6. Serve.

 # CHIPOTLE CHICKEN MELTDOWN

Serving size- 1 party platter

Ingredients:
6 (8oz) boneless skinless chicken breasts (thinly pounded and cut in half)
3/4 cup mayonnaise
1 tablespoon finely chopped chipotle peppers (canned)
2 pinch's pepper
1 pinch salt
2 cups unseasoned breadcrumbs
cooking spray
12 slices swiss cheese

Method:
1. Preheat oven 350°F.
2. In a large mixing bowl, combine mayonnaise, chipotle peppers, pepper and salt. Mix well.
3. Smother chicken breasts with mayonnaise mixture then coat in breadcrumbs.
4. Place chicken on a sprayed baking sheet.
5. Bake chicken for about 30-35 minutes.
6. Place slice of swiss cheese on each chicken breast and bake another 5 minutes.
7. Serve.

 # HONEY FRIED CHICKEN DRUMSTICKS

Serving size- 1 party basket

Ingredients:
3 lbs chicken drumsticks
3 cups buttermilk
1/2 cup honey
oil for frying
2 cups unbleached flour
1/4 cup finely chopped fresh parsley
2 tablespoons ground mustard
1 tablespoon paprika
1 tablespoon garlic powder
1 teaspoon pepper
1 teaspoon salt

Method:
1. Place chicken, buttermilk and honey in a large zip-lock bag. Shake well and refrigerate for 24 hours.
2. Pour oil in a large stockpot until 1/2 full. Heat to 370°F.
3. In a large mixing bowl, combine flour, parsley, mustard, paprika, garlic powder, pepper and salt. Mix well.
4. Remove chicken from zip-lock bag and dredge in flour. Coat well.
5. Fry chicken drumsticks for about 8-10 minutes. Remove from oil and pat dry.
6. Serve.

CLASSY CHICKEN CORDON BLEU
(with a tarragon cream sauce)

Serving size- 1 party platter, 12 cordon blue

Ingredients:
6 (8oz) boneless skinless chicken breasts (thinly pounded and cut in half)
12 slices honey ham deli meat
12 slices swiss cheese
24 asparagus spears (blanched and chilled)
1 cup unseasoned breadcrumbs
12 toothpicks
3 tablespoons extra virgin olive oil

Method:
1. Preheat oven 375°F.
2. Place one slice of ham and swiss cheese on each piece of chicken. Place two asparagus spears on top of cheese.
3. Roll chicken tight from one end to the other.
4. Coat chicken in breadcrumbs. Stick toothpicks through the center of the chicken.
5. Place chicken on a baking sheet and drizzle with olive oil.
6. Bake chicken for about 30-35 minutes. Remove from oven. Serve with sauce.

Tarragon Cream Sauce

Ingredients:
2 tablespoons extra virgin olive oil
1/2 small finely diced red onion
1 tablespoon finely chopped fresh tarragon leaves
1/4 cup chicken broth
3/4 cup heavy cream
2 pinch's pepper
1 pinch salt

Method:
1. Drizzle olive oil in a small saucepot over medium heat.
2. Sauté onions for about 5 minutes, stirring occasionally.
3. Add all other ingredients and lower heat to a simmer and cook for about 15-20 minutes until sauce starts to thicken.
4. Serve.

PISTACHIO CRUSTED CHICKEN
(With a cranberry honey Dijon sauce)

Serving size- 1 party platter

Ingredients:
6 (8oz) boneless skinless chicken breasts (thinly pounded and cut in half)
1/2 cup ground pistachios
1/2 cup unseasoned breadcrumbs
3 tablespoons extra virgin olive oil

Method:
1. Preheat oven 350°F.
2. In a large mixing bowl, combine ground pistachios and breadcrumbs. Mix well.
3. Coat each piece of chicken with breadcrumb mixture.
4. Place chicken on a baking sheet and drizzle with olive oil.
5. Bake chicken for about 25-30 minutes. Remove from oven. Serve with sauce.

Cranberry Honey Dijon Sauce:

Ingredients:
1 cup canned cranberry sauce
3 tablespoons Dijon mustard
2 tablespoons honey
2 pinch's pepper
1 pinch salt

Method:
1. Place all ingredients in a food processor and puree until smooth and creamy.
2. Serve.

CHICKEN LEMONCELLO

Serving size- 1 party platter

Ingredients:
3 tablespoons extra virgin olive oil
6 (8oz) boneless skinless chicken breasts (thinly pounded and cut in half)
1/2 cup all-purpose flour
1/2 cup white wine
1/4 cup lemoncello liquor
1/2 cup butter
2 tablespoons capers
1 tablespoon finely chopped fresh parsley
2 pinch's pepper
1 pinch salt

Method:
1. Drizzle olive oil in a large skillet over medium heat.
2. Lightly flour each piece of chicken. Remove any excess flour.
3. Place chicken breast in skillet and cook for about 5-6 minutes. Turn chicken and cook for another 5 minutes.
4. Remove skillet from heat and add wine and lemoncello. Place skillet back on heat. Cook for another 2-3 minutes. Remove from heat and add all other ingredients. Keep stirring until butter becomes a nice smooth sauce.
5. Serve.

BAKED STUFFED CHICKEN MARSALA

Serving size- 8 stuffed chicken breasts

Ingredients:
3 tablespoons extra virgin olive oil
1 small finely diced white onion
1 cup domestic mushrooms (sliced)
1 cup shitaki mushrooms (stems removed and chopped)
1 cup crimini mushrooms (sliced)
1/2 cup unseasoned breadcrumbs
2 pinch's pepper
1 pinch salt
8 (8oz) boneless, skin on chicken breast (thinly pounded)

Method:
1. Preheat oven 350°F.
2. Drizzle olive oil in a large skillet over medium heat.
3. Sauté onions and all three mushrooms for 5 minutes, stirring occasionally. Remove from heat.
4. Place mushroom mixture in a food processor and puree.
5. In a large mixing bowl, combine mushroom puree, breadcrumbs, pepper and salt. Mix well.
6. Place chicken breast skin side down on a baking sheet.
7. Place equal amounts of mushroom mixture in center of chicken breast. Pull sides of chicken breast up and over the mushrooms mixture to form a ball. Turn chicken over.
8. Bake chicken for about 30-35 minutes. Remove from oven.
9. Serve with sauce.

(con't. pg. 129)

Marsala Sauce

Ingredients:
2 tablespoons extra virgin olive oil
1/2 small finely diced red onion
1/4 cup marsala wine
1/2 cup chicken broth
1/4 cup butter
2 pinch's pepper
1 pinch salt

Method:
1. Drizzle olive oil in a small saucepot over medium heat.
2. Sauté onions for 5 minutes, stirring occasionally.
3. Remove sauce from heat. Add marsala wine. Return saucepot to heat and cook for 2-3 minutes. Add chicken broth and cook for 5 minutes.
4. Remove from heat and add all other ingredients. Keep stirring until butter becomes a nice smooth sauce. Serve.

CHICKEN WELLINGTON

Serving size- 1 party platter, 6 wellingtons

Ingredients:
3 tablespoons extra virgin olive oil
6 (8oz) boneless skinless chicken breasts (thinly pounded & cut in half)
1/2 cup all-purpose flour
1 sheet thawed puff pastry (store bought)
6 tablespoons boursin cheese
6 slices honey ham deli meat
cooking spray

Method:
1. Preheat oven 400°F.
2. Drizzle olive oil in a large skillet.
3. Lightly flour each chicken breast. Remove any excess flour.
4. Place chicken breast in skillet and cook for about 5-6 minutes. Turn chicken over and cook another 5 minutes. Remove from heat.
5. Cut puff pastry into 6 equal squares.
6. Place one chicken breast in the center of each puff pastry square. Top each one with one-tablespoon of cheese, one slice of another chicken breast. Pull edges of the pastry up and over the top of the chicken breast. Turn Wellington over.
7. Place Wellingtons on a sprayed baking sheet.
8. Bake Wellington for about 30-35 minutes until golden brown. Remove from oven and serve.

BAKED STUFFED CHICKEN PARMESAN
(with marinara sauce)

Serving size- 1 party platter-6 stuffed chicken breasts

Ingredients:
6 (8oz) boneless skinless chicken breasts (thinly pounded & cut in half)
1/2 cup all-purpose flour
3 large eggs
1 cup 1/2 & 1/2
1 cup Italian seasoned breadcrumbs
1/4 cup extra virgin olive oil
1 cup ricotta cheese
1 tablespoon dried oregano
1 teaspoon garlic
1 teaspoon onion powder
1/4 teaspoon pepper
1/4 teaspoon salt
1 batch marinara sauce (see pg. 132)
1 cup shredded mozzarella cheese

Method:
1. Preheat oven 350°F.
2. Lightly flour chicken breast.
3. In a large mixing bowl, beat eggs and 1/2 & 1/2. Beat well.
4. Dip floured chicken in egg mixture and then coat in breadcrumbs. Set aside.
5. Drizzle olive oil in a large skillet over medium heat.
6. Place breaded chicken in skillet and cook for about 5-6 minutes, turn chicken over and cook for another 5 minutes. Remove from heat.
7. In a large mixing bowl, combine ricotta cheese, oregano, garlic powder, onion powder, pepper and salt. Mix well.
8. Place 6 pieces of chicken in a casserole dish, place equal amounts of ricotta cheese mixture on top of chicken. Then place 6 other chicken breasts on top of ricotta cheese. Top with sauce and shredded mozzarella cheese.
9. Bake casserole for about 20-25 minutes.
10. Serve.

 # MARINARA SAUCE

Serving size- 1 batch

Ingredients:
1/4 cup extra virgin olive oil
1 tablespoon fresh chopped garlic
3 cups canned crushed tomatoes
1 tablespoon dried oregano
1 teaspoon garlic powder
1/4 teaspoon pepper
1/4 teaspoon salt

Method:
1. Drizzle olive oil in a medium saucepot over medium heat.
2. Sauté garlic for about 2-3 minutes, stirring frequently.
3. Add all other ingredients and lower heat to a simmer. Continue cooking for about 30 minutes.
4. Serve.

GRILLED TURKEY TIPS

Serving size- 1 party platter

Ingredients:
3 lbs turkey tenderloins (cut into 2" pieces)
1/2 cup extra virgin olive oil
2 tablespoons Dijon mustard
1 tablespoon fresh chopped garlic
1 small finely diced red onion
1 tablespoon finely chopped fresh parsley
1/4 teaspoon pepper
1/4 teaspoon salt

Method:
1. Place all ingredients in a large zip-lock bag. Shake well. Refrigerate for about 24 hours.
2. Preheat grill to a medium high heat.
3. Remove turkey tips from marinade and grill for about 5-6 minutes. Turn tips over and grill another 5 minutes. Remove from grill.
4. Serve.

Beef, Pork and Lamb

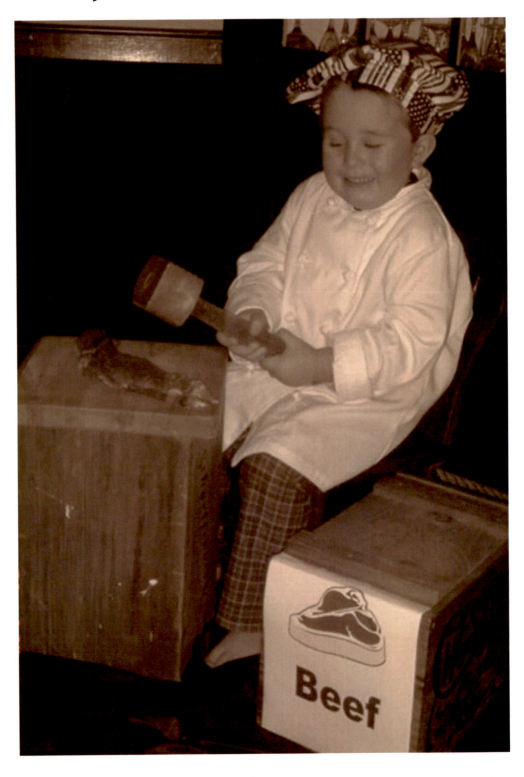

COFFEE CRUSTED SIRLOIN STEAKS
(with a coconut lime butter)

Serving size-1 party platter, 6 steaks

Ingredients:
3 tablespoons extra virgin olive oil
6 (12oz) sirloin steaks
1 cup coffee grounds
1/2 cup canned pimentos (chopped)
1/4 cup lime juice
3/4 cup canned cream of coconut
1/4 cup butter
2 pinch's pepper
1 pinch salt

Method:
1. Drizzle olive oil in a large skillet over medium heat.
2. Coat each sirloin steak with coffee grounds.
3. Place steaks in skillet and cook for about 6-7 minutes. Turn steaks over and cook another 6 minutes.
4. Add chopped pimentos, lime juice and cream of coconut. Cook for 3-4 minutes.
5. Remove skillet from heat and add all other ingredients. Keep stirring until butter becomes a nice smooth sauce.
6. Serve.

FORTY-EIGHT HOUR SIRLOIN TIPS

Serving size- 1 party platter

Ingredients:
3 lbs sirloin tip meat (cut into 2" pieces)
2 cups coca cola
1/2 cup teriyaki
1/2 cup extra virgin olive oil
1/4 teaspoon crushed red pepper flakes
2 tablespoons fresh chopped garlic
2 pinch's pepper
1 pinch salt

Method:
1. Place all ingredients in a large zip-lock bag. Shake well. Refrigerate for 48 hours.
2. Preheat grill to a medium-high heat.
3. Remove steak from marinade.
4. Grill steak tips for about 6 minutes. Turn tips over and cook for another 6 minutes.
5. Serve.

SEARED FILET MIGNON
(with a gorgonzola & bacon steak butter)

Serving size-1 party platter, 6 steaks

Ingredients:
2 tablespoons extra virgin olive oil
6 (8oz) filet mignon steaks
2 pinch's pepper
1 pinch salt
1/2 cup cooked chopped bacon
1 tablespoon Worcestershire sauce
3/4 cup butter (softened)
4 oz crumbled gorgonzola cheese
1/4 cup fresh chopped shallots
2 tablespoons finely chopped fresh parsley

Method:
1. Drizzle olive oil in a large skillet over medium heat.
2. Season steaks with pepper and salt.
3. Place steaks in skillet and cook for 6-7 minutes. Turn steaks over and cook another 6 minutes.
4. Add bacon. Cook for about 5 minutes, stirring frequently.
5. Remove skillet from heat, add all other ingredients and keep stirring until butter becomes a nice smooth sauce.
6. Serve.

STUFFED CHOPPED SIRLOIN STEAKS
(with a mushroom cream sauce)

Serving size - 1 party platter, 6 steaks

Ingredients:
3 tablespoons extra virgin olive oil
2 lbs ground sirloin
1 small finely diced white onion
1 tablespoon garlic powder
1 tablespoon onion powder
1 tablespoon finely chopped fresh parsley
1/2 cup boursin cheese
2 tablespoons butter
1 cup domestic mushrooms (sliced)
3/4 cup heavy cream
1 tablespoon finely chopped fresh parsley
2 pinch's pepper
1 pinch salt

Method:
1. Drizzle olive oil in a large skillet over medium heat.
2. In a large mixing bowl, combine sirloin, onions, garlic powder, onion powder and parsley. Mix well.
3. Divide sirloin mixture into 6 equal portions. Stuff sirloin mixture with equal portions of boursin cheese and form into patties.
4. Place patties in skillet and cook for about 6-7 minutes. Turn patties over and cook another 6 minutes.
5. Add butter and mushrooms to skillet. Cook for another 3-4 minutes.
6. Add all other ingredients and cook for another 4-5 minutes.
7. Serve.

 # CARMELIZED ONION MEAT LOAF

Serving size- 1 large loaf

Ingredients:
2 tablespoons butter
2 large finely diced white onions
2 tablespoons brown sugar
3 lbs ground beef (85% lean)
3/4 cup mayonnaise
4 large eggs
6 slices white sandwich bread (diced)
1 tablespoon onion powder
1 teaspoon garlic powder
1 tablespoon finely chopped fresh parlsey
1 teaspoon pepper
1 teaspoon salt

Method:
1. Preheat oven 350°F.
2. Melt butter in a large skillet over high heat.
3. Sauté onions for about 8-10 minutes, stirring occasionally. Add brown sugar and cook another 5 minutes. Remove from heat.
4. In a large mixing bowl, combine onions and all other ingredients. Mix well.
5. Place meatloaf mixture into a loaf pan and press down firmly.
6. Bake meatloaf for about 40-45 minutes. Remove from oven.
7. Slice and serve.

SPICY PINEAPPLE BRAISED BEEF SHORT RIBS

Serving size- 1 party platter

Ingredients:
1/4 cup extra virgin olive oil
4 lbs beef short ribs
1 cup all-purpose flour
4 cups beef broth
1 cup canned crushed pineapple
1/4 cup brown sugar
1 cup pineapple juice
1/2 teaspoon crushed red pepper flakes
1 teaspoon pepper
1 teaspoon salt

Method:
1. Preheat oven 375°F.
2. Drizzle olive oil in a large skillet over high heat.
3. Lightly flour ribs. Remove any excess flour.
4. Place ribs in skillet and cook for 5 minutes. Turn ribs over and cook another 5 minutes.
5. Add all other ingredients to skillet and cover with aluminum foil.
6. Bake skillet for 2 hours. Remove from oven.
7. Serve.

GARLIC CRUSTED SIRLOIN STEAKS

Serving size- 1 party platter, 6 steaks

Ingredients:
3 tablespoons extra virgin olive oil
6 (12oz) sirloin steaks
2 pinch's pepper
1 pinch salt
1 cup unseasoned breadcrumbs
1/4 cup butter (melted)
1 tablespoon fresh chopped garlic
1 tablespoon finely chopped fresh parsley

Method:
1. Preheat oven 375°F.
2. Drizzle olive oil in a large skillet over medium heat.
3. Season steaks with pepper and salt.
4. Place steaks in skillet and cook for about 4 minutes. Turn steaks over and cook another 4 minutes. Remove skillet from heat.
5. In a small mixing bowl, combine all other ingredients. Mix well.
6. Place breadcrumb mixture on top of each steak and press down firmly.
7. Place skillet in oven and bake for 10 minutes.
8. Serve.

DIJON CRUSTED PORK CHOPS

Serving size- 1 party platter, 6 chops

Ingredients:
3 tablespoons extra virgin olive oil
6 (double thick) center cut pork chops
1/2 cup all-purpose flour
1 cup unseasoned breadcrumbs
3 tablespoons Dijon mustard
3 tablespoons butter (melted)
1 teaspoon finely chopped fresh rosemary leaves

Method:
1. Preheat oven 350°F.
2. Drizzle olive oil in a large skillet over medium heat.
3. Lightly flour pork chops. Remove excess flour.
4. Place pork chops in skillet and cook for about 5 minutes. Turn chops over and cook another 5 minutes. Remove skillet from heat.
5. In a small mixing bowl, combine all other ingredients. Mix well.
6. Place breadcrumb mixture on top of each chop and press down firmly.
7. Place skillet in oven and bake for 20 minutes.
8. Serve.

 # APPLE ROASTED PORK LOIN

Serving size - 1 party platter, 1 roast

Ingredients:
1 (4-5 lb) center cut pork loin roast
1 large finely sliced white onion
1 teaspoon finely chopped fresh sage leaves
2 tablespoons fresh chopped garlic
1 cup canned apple sauce
1/4 cup apple juice
1/4 cup extra virgin olive oil
2 tablespoons apple cider vinegar
1/2 teaspoon pepper
1 teaspoon salt

Method:
1. Place all ingredients in a large zip-lock bag. Shake well. Refrigerate for about 24 hours.
2. Preheat oven 350°F.
3. Remove pork loin from marinade and place on baking sheet.
4. Bake pork loin for about 1 hour 15 minutes. Remove from oven.
5. Slice and serve.

GRILLED HERBED MARINATED LAMBCHOPS
(with a mint & lime yogurt sauce)

Serving size -1 party platter, 12 chops

Ingredients:
12 (5oz) baby lamb chops
2 tablespoons finely chopped fresh mint leaves
1 tablespoon finely chopped fresh rosemary leaves
2 tablespoons fresh chopped garlic
3/4 cup extra virgin olive oil
1/2 teaspoon pepper
1/2 teaspoon salt

Method:
1. Place all ingredients in a large zip-lock bag. Shake well. Refrigerate for 24 hours.
2. Preheat grill to a medium-high heat.
3. Remove lamb chops from marinade.
4. Grill chops for about 7-8 minutes. Turn chops over and grill another 7 minutes.
5. Serve with sauce.

Mint & lime yogurt sauce.

Ingredients:
1 cup plain yogurt
1/4 cup lime juice
2 tablespoons finely chopped fresh mint leaves
2 pinch's pepper
1 pinch salt

Method:
1. Place all ingredients in a food processor and puree until smooth and creamy.
2. Serve.

LAMB BOLOGNESE

Serving size: 1 party casserole

Ingredients:
2 tablespoons vegetable oil
1 pinch salt
1 lb dried linguini pasta
3 tablespoons extra virgin olive oil
2 lbs fresh ground lamb
1 large finely diced red bell pepper
1 large finely diced green bell pepper
1 large finely diced red onion
1 tablespoon fresh chopped garlic
3 cups canned crushed tomatoes
2 tablespoons dried oregano
1 tablespoon garlic powder
1 teaspoon pepper
1 teaspoon salt
1/2 cup grated romano cheese

Method:
1. Preheat oven 350°F.
2. Bring pot of water to a boil. Drizzle vegetable oil and pinch of salt into water. Cook linguini until just tender. Drain and cool.
3. Drizzle olive oil in a large stockpot over medium heat.
4. Sauté ground lamb, red peppers, green peppers, red onion and garlic. Cover and sauté for about 10-12 minutes, stirring frequently.
5. Uncover and add all other ingredients except romano cheese. Mix well.
6. Reduce heat to a simmer and cook for another 30 minutes. Add linguini. Mix well.
7. Place in casserole dish.
8. Bake casserole for about 15 minutes. Remove from oven.
9. Sprinkle with romano cheese and serve.

Sunday Brunch

AFTERNOON FRUIT SALAD

Serving size - 1 party bowl

Ingredients:
1 small pineapple (diced)
1 small cantalope melon (diced)
1 small honeydew melon (diced)
4 red delicious apples (diced)
2 lbs red grapes (removed from stems)
2 lbs green grapes (removed from stems)
1 tablespoon finely chopped fresh mint leaves
1 cup vanilla yogurt
2 tablespoons honey

Method:
1. In a large mixing bowl, combine all ingredients. Mix well.
2. Refrigerate salad for about 2 hours
3. Serve.

SMOKED SALMON CREAM CHEESE SPREAD
(with fried bagel chips)

Serving size-1 party platter

Ingredients:
oil for frying
6 large plain bagels (thinly sliced)
2 pinch's kosher salt
1 lb cream cheese (softened)
10 ozs sliced smoked salmon (chopped)
1 tablespoon finely chopped fresh parsley
1 teaspoon finely chopped fresh dill
1 pinch pepper

Method:
1. Pour oil in a large stockpot until ½ full and heat to 370°F.
2. Fry bagel chips for about 4-5 minutes until golden brown. Remove from oil and pat dry. Season with kosher salt. Serve in a basket.
3. Place all other ingredients in a food processor and puree until smooth and creamy.
4. Refrigerate cheese spread for about 1 hour.
5. Serve with bagel chips.

SPICY SCRAMBLED EGGS
(martini style)

Serving size - 1 large martini glass

Ingredients:
2 tablespoons butter
1/2 cup fresh chopped scallions
1/2 cup canned green olives (pitted & chopped)
1/2 cup canned black olives (pitted & chopped)
1/2 cup canned pimentos (chopped)
1 tablespoon vodka
8 large eggs
1/4 cup heavy cream
1 tablespoon finely chopped fresh parsley
2 pinch's pepper
1 pinch salt
1/2 cup shredded cheddar cheese

Method:
1. Melt butter in a large skillet over medium heat.
2. Sauté scallions, green olives, black olives and pimentos for about 5 minutes, stirring occasionally.
3. Remove skillet from heat and add vodka. Return back to heat and sauté another 2-3 minutes.
4. In a large mixing bowl, beat eggs, heavy cream, parsley, pepper and salt together.
5. Add egg mixture to skillet and stir frequently until eggs are nice and fluffy. Remove from heat and stir in cheddar cheese.
6. Serve in a large martini glass.

BREAKFAST QUESADILLA

Serving size-1 party platter, about 15-20 pieces

Ingredients:
2 tablespoons butter
1 small finely diced red bell pepper
1 small finely diced red onion
1/2 cup finely diced plum tomatoes
6 large eggs
1/4 cup heavy cream
2 pinch's pepper
1 pinch salt
4 12" flour tortillas
1 cup shredded pepper jack cheese

Method:
1. Preheat oven 400°F.
2. Melt butter in a large skillet over medium heat.
3. Sauté red peppers, green peppers, red onions and tomatoes for about 5 minutes, stirring occasionally.
4. In a large mixing bowl, beat eggs, heavy cream, pepper and salt together.
5. Add egg mixture to skillet and stir frequently until eggs are nice and fluffy. Remove from heat.
6. Divide the egg mixture equally over the tortillas. Spread the pepper jack cheese over egg mixture and fold tortillas in half.
7. Place on baking sheet and bake for about 10-12 minutes until tortillas are brown and crispy. Cut tortillas into 4-5 pieces.
8. Serve.

EGGNOG FRENCH TOAST

Serving size-1 party platter, 16 triangles

Ingredients:
3 tablespoons butter
8 slices thick sour dough bread
1 pint eggnog
4 large eggs
1 tablespoon brandy
1 teaspoon ground cinnamon
(garnish) powdered sugar
(garnish) maple syrup

Method:
1. Melt butter in a large skillet over medium heat.
2. In a large mixing bowl, beat eggnog, eggs, brandy and ground cinnamon together.
3. Dip bread into egg mixture and place in skillet. Cook for about 5-6 minutes. Turn French toast over and cook another 5 minutes until golden brown.
4. Serve with powdered sugar and maple syrup.

CREOLE OMELET

Serving size- 1 party omelet

Ingredients:
3 tablespoon butter
1 small finely diced red bell pepper
1 small finely diced green bell pepper
1 small finely diced red onion
1 lb cooked crawfish meat
1/2 teaspoon fresh chopped garlic
6 large eggs
1/2 cup heavy cream
1 teaspoon Cajun seasoning
1/2 cup canned crushed tomatoes
1 cup shredded Monterey Jack Cheese

Method:
1. Melt butter in a large skillet over medium heat.
2. Sauté red peppers, green peppers, red onions, crawfish meat and garlic for about 5 minutes, stirring occasionally.
3. In a large mixing bowl, beat eggs, heavy cream, Cajun seasoning and canned crushed tomatoes together.
4. Add egg mixture to skillet with a rubber spatula. Push the cooked edges toward the center while keeping the eggs in an even layer. Flip omelet over and cook for about 2-3 minutes. Top with shredded cheese and fold in half.
S5. lide omelet on platter and serve.

 # OLD FASHIONED HOME FRIES

Serving size-1 party bowl

Ingredients:
3 lbs red bliss potatoes (washed and quartered)
3 tablespoons extra virgin olive oil
1 large finely diced white onion
1 tablespoon finely chopped fresh parsley
1 teaspoon finely chopped fresh sage leaves
1 teaspoon onion powder
1 teaspoon garlic powder
1 teaspoon pepper
1 teaspoon salt

Method:
1. Place potatoes in a pot of water. Boil potatoes until fork tender. Drain and cool.
2. Drizzle olive oil in a large skillet over medium heat.
3. Sauté onions for about 5 minutes, stirring occasionally. Add potatoes and all other ingredients. Cook for another 10 minutes, stirring frequently.
4. Serve.

OSCAR BENEDICT
(with a dill hollandaise sauce)

Serving Size: 1 party platter, 12 benedicts

Ingredients:
1/2 cup white vinegar
1 tablespoon extra virgin olive oil
1 small finely diced red onion
1 bunch asparagus spears (blanched, chilled & diced)
1 cup fresh cooked lobster meat (chopped)
12 eggs
6 English muffins (split)

Method:
1. Bring pot of water to a boil. Lower heat to medium and add vinegar.
2. Drizzle olive oil in a large skillet over medium heat.
3. Sauté onions for about 5 minutes, stirring occasionally. Stir in asparagus and lobster meat. Cook another 5 minutes and remove from heat.
4. Crack eggs in the pot of water and poach for about 5-6 minutes, until egg whites are nice and firm.
5. Toast English muffins and place on platter.
6. Top English muffins with equal amounts of asparagus mixture, then top each muffin with one egg and dill hollandaise sauce.
7. Serve.

(con't. pg. 155)

Dill Hollandaise sauce

Ingredients:
1/2 cup butter
2 egg yolks
2 teaspoons lemon juice
1 pinch cayenne pepper
1 pinch pepper
1 pinch salt
1 splash white wine
1 splash water
2 teaspoons Worcestershire sauce
1 teaspoon finely chopped fresh dill

Method:
1. In a small saucepot, melt butter until hot. Set aside
2. Add all other ingredients except dill in a double boiler and whisk over high heat until thickened.
3. Remove from heat and slowly add melted butter while whisking. Add chopped dill.

SMOKED SALMON PINWHEELS

Serving size- 1 party platter

Ingredients:
2 large rectangular flat breads
1/2 cup sour cream
1 tablespoon lemon juice
2 tablespoons capers
2 tablespoons finely chopped fresh dill
2 pinch's pepper
2 lbs sliced smoked salmon
2 cups mixed field greens

Method:
1. In a small mixing bowl, combine sour cream, lemon juice, capers, dill and pepper. Mix well.
2. Spread sour cream mixture evenly over the two flat breads.
3. Top with sliced smoked salmon and field greens.
4. Roll flat bread tightly. Cut 1" slices out of flat bread logs.
5. Serve on a platter.

BLUEBERRY BROWN SUGAR PANCAKES

Serving size-1 party stack

Ingredients:
2 cups all-purpose flour
2 tablespoons brown sugar
2 teaspoons baking powder
1 1/2 teaspoons baking soda
1/2 teaspoon salt
2 large eggs
1 3/4 cup milk
2 tablespoons butter (melted)
1/2 cup fresh blueberries
3 tablespoons butter
(garnish) powdered sugar
(garnish) maple syrup

Method:
1. In a large mixing bowl, sift flour, brown sugar, baking powder, baking soda and salt.
2. In another large mixing bowl, beat eggs, milk and butter together, slowly add flour mixture to egg mixture. Fold in blueberries.
3. Melt butter on a griddle over medium heat.
4. Pour equal amounts of pancake batter on the griddle and cook until pancake batter starts to get bubbles. Flip pancakes over and cook until golden brown.
5. Serve with powdered sugar and maple syrup.

DOUBLE BITE MONTE CRISTO

Serving size- 8 triangle sandwiches

Ingredients:
8 slices white sandwich bread
1/2 lb sliced ham deli meat
1/2 lb sliced roasted turkey deli meat
4 slices swiss cheese
1/2 cup raspberry preserve (store bought)
3 tablespoons butter
4 large eggs
1 cup milk
(garnish) powdered sugar

Method:
1. Preheat oven 375°F.
2. Place slices of ham, turkey and swiss cheese on four slices of bread. Spread raspberry preserves on top of meats and cheese. Top with the other four slices of bread.
3. Melt butter in a large skillet over medium heat.
4. In a large mixing bowl, beat eggs and milk together.
5. Dip sandwiches in egg mixture and place in skillet. Cook for about 5 minutes. Flip sandwiches over and place in oven for about 5-6 minutes until golden brown. Remove from oven.
6. Cut sandwiches in half on an angle.
7. Serve.

Sweet Endings

HOMEMADE WHIPPED CREAM

Serving size- 1 bowl

Ingredients:
1 quart extra heavy cream
1 cup powdered sugar
1 tablespoon vanilla extract

Method:
1. Place all ingredients in a mixer. Cover with cloth and mix on high speed until cream is nice and thick.

 # BEST EVER HOT FUDGE

Serving size- 1 bowl

Ingredients:
1 cup heavy cream
4 cups semi-sweet chocolate chips
1 tablespoon vanilla extract
1 tablespoon butter

Method:
1. Place all ingredients in a small saucepot over low heat.
2. Stir ingredients with a whisk until melted together.
3. Serve.

WHITE CHOCOLATE FONDUE
(with strawberry skewers)

Serving size- 1 party platter

Ingredients:
1 cup heavy cream
6 cups white chocolate chips
1 tablespoon vanilla extract
6" wooden skewers
2 quarts fresh strawberries

Method:
1. Place heavy cream, white chocolate chips and vanilla in a small saucepot over low heat.
2. Stir ingredients with a whisk until melted together. Remove from heat and serve in a bowl.
3. Place skewers through the center of strawberries. Serve on a platter.

MARSHMALLOW PARFAIT

Serving size- 1 glass bowl

Ingredients:
1 quart heavy cream
1/2 cup raspberry preserve (store bought)
4 cups mini marshmallows
1/4 cup raspberry liquor
2 pints fresh raspberries
(garnish) homemade whipped cream

Method:
1. In a large mixing bowl, whisk heavy cream and raspberry preserve together until smooth and creamy.
2. Fold marshmallows, raspberry liquor and raspberries into cream mixture.
3. Place mixture in a large glass bowl and cover with plastic wrap.
4. Refrigerate bowl for 24 hours.
5. Serve with homemade whipped cream.

DOUBLE CHOCOLATE WOOPIE PIES

Serving size- 1 party platter, about 12-15 woopie pies

Ingredients:
1/2 cup shortening
1 cup granulated sugar
2 large eggs
1 teaspoon vanilla extract
2 cups all-purpose flour
1 1/2 teaspoons baking soda
1/2 teaspoon baking powder
1/2 teaspoon salt
1/2 cup cocoa powder
1 cup milk

Method:
1. Preheat oven 375°F.
2. In a large mixing bowl, cream together shortening and sugar until fluffy and creamy. Add eggs one at a time. Add vanilla and set aside.
3. In another large mixing bowl, sift together flour, baking soda, baking powder, salt and cocoa powder.
4. Add dry ingredients into wet ingredients. Slowly add milk. Mix well.
5. Drop round teaspoonfuls onto un-greased cookie sheets.
6. Bake cookie sheets for 7-10 minutes. Remove and cool.
7. Scoop filing on top of 1/2 the rounds, place other 1/2 of rounds on top of filling to form woopie pies.
8. Serve.

Filling:
3/4 cup shortening
2 1/4 cup powdered sugar
1 13oz jar marshmallow fluff (store bought)
1/2 teaspoon vanilla extract
2 tablespoons cocoa powder

Method:
1. In a large mixing bowl, cream shortening, add powdered sugar, marshmallow fluff, vanilla and cocoa powder one at a time. Mix well.
2. Ready to use.

BLUEBERRY CRUMBLE

Serving size- 1 baking dish

Ingredients:
4 pints fresh blueberries
1 cup blueberry preserves (store bought)
1 cup sugar
2 tablespoons lemon juice
1/4 cup butter (softened)
3/4 cup all-purpose flour
1/2 cup sugar
1 pinch salt
(garnish) vanilla ice-cream

Method:
1. Preheat oven 350°F.
2. In a large mixing bowl, combine blueberries, blueberry preserves, 1 cup sugar and lemon juice. Mix well.
3. Place blueberry mixture in a baking dish. Set aside.
4. In a large mixing bowl, combine butter, flour, sugar and salt. Cover the blueberry mixture with crumble mixture.
5. Bake baking dish for about 40 minutes until golden brown.
6. Serve with ice-cream.

CHOCOLATE CHIP OATMEAL DROP COOKIES

Serving size- 1 party platter, about 3 dozen cookies

Ingredients:
2 cup all purpose flour
1 teaspoon baking soda
1 teaspoon salt
1 1/2 teaspoon ground cinnamon
2 cups oatmeal
1 cup butter (softened)
1/2 cup granulated sugar
3/4 cup brown sugar
2 large eggs
1/2 teaspoon vanilla extract
1/4 cup & 2 tablespoons milk
1 cup raisins
1 cup semi-sweet chocolate chips
 cooking spray

Method:
1. Preheat oven 375°F.
2. In a large mixing bowl, sift flour, baking soda, salt and cinnamon. Add oatmeal.
3. In another large mixing bowl, cream together butter, sugar, eggs and vanilla. Beat until smooth and creamy. Slowly add milk and mix well.
4. Add dry ingredients into wet ingredients. Mix well.
5. Fold raisins and chocolate chips into cookie batter.
6. Spray cookie sheet with cooking spray.
7. Drop round teaspoonfuls on cookie sheet.
8. Bake cookie sheets for about 12 minutes or until golden brown.
9. Remove from oven and cool.
10. Serve.

CHOCOLATE SNOWBALLS

Serving size- 1 party platter, 8 large snowballs

Ingredients:
1 quart chocolate ice-cream
1 cup shredded coconut
2 cups chocolate cookie crumbs
(garnish) best ever hot fudge

Method:
1. Scoop ice cream into 8 large balls and freeze for 1 hour.
2. In a large mixing bowl, combine coconut and cookie crumbs together. Mix well.
3. Roll each ice cream ball in cookie mixture.
4. Serve on a platter with best ever hot fudge.

ROCKY ROAD CHEESECAKE

Serving size- 1 cheesecake

Ingredients:
1 cup chocolate cookie crumbs
3 tablespoons melted butter
cooking spray
24 oz cream cheese (softened)
1 cup granulated sugar
6 large eggs
1 tablespoon vanilla extract
2 tablespoons cocoa powder
1 pinch salt
1 cup semi-sweet chocolate chips
1/4 cup chopped walnuts
1 cup mini-marshmallows

Method:
1. Preheat oven 375°F.
2. In a small mixing bowl, combine cookie crumbs and butter. Mix well.
3. Spray 9" spring form pan with cooking spray.
4. Spread cookie mixture evenly on bottom of spring form pan. Set a side.
5. In a large mixing bowl, beat cream cheese and sugar together until creamy and smooth. Mix eggs into cream cheese mixture one at a time on low speed. Add vanilla, cocoa and salt. Mix well.
6. Fold chocolate chips, walnuts and marshmallows into cheesecake batter.
7. Pour cheesecake batter into spring form pan over cookie crumbs.
8. Bake cheesecake for about 1-1 hour 15 minutes. Remove from oven and cool.
9. Refrigerate cheesecake for about 24 hours.
10. Serve.

SUGAR COATED FRIED FLOUR TORTILLAS
(with strawberry pico di galo sauce)

Serving size- 1 party platter

Ingredients:
oil for frying
6 12" flour tortillas (cut into small triangle pieces)
2 tablespoons granulated sugar
2 tablespoons powdered sugar
1/4 teaspoon ground cinnamon

Method:
1. Pour oil in a large stockpot until 1/2 full and heat oil to 370°F.
2. Fry tortillas for about 4-5 minutes until golden brown. Remove tortillas from oil and pat dry.
3. In a large mixing bowl, combine granulated sugar, powdered sugar and cinnamon together. Mix well. Add tortillas and toss.
4. Serve on a platter.

Strawberry Pico Di Galo Sauce

Ingredients:
1 pint fresh strawberries (sliced)
1 tablespoon finely chopped fresh mint leaves
1 tablespoon fresh chopped scallions
1 teaspoon Tabasco
1 teaspoon honey

Method:
1. Place all ingredients in a food processor and pulse. You don't want to puree the sauce. You want it to be a little chunky.
2. Serve in a bowl with tortillas.

APPLE CINNAMON WONTONS

Serving size- 15 wontons

Ingredients:
oil for frying
2 tablespoons butter
5 granny smith apples (peeled and finely diced)
1 teaspoon ground cinnamon
1/4 cup raisins
15 wonton wrappers
3 large eggs (beaten)
2 tablespoons granulated sugar

Method:
1. Pour oil in a large stockpot until 1/2 full and heat to 370°F.
2. Melt butter in a large skillet over medium heat.
3. Sauté apples for about 5 minutes, stirring occasionally. Add cinnamon and raisins. Mix well. Remove from heat and cool.
4. Brush beaten eggs over the top of wontons. Scoop equal amounts of apple mixture in center of wontons. Fold one corner of wontons to the other corner to form a triangle, press down firmly on edges of wonton.
5. Fry wontons for about 4-5 minutes until golden brown and crispy. Remove from oil and pat dry.
6. Toss with granulated sugar.
7. Serve.

THREE BERRY PASTRY PILLOWS

Serving size- 1 party platter, 12 pillows

Ingredients:
2 sheets thawed puff pastry (each sheet cut into 6 equal squares)
cooking spray
1 pint fresh strawberries (sliced)
1 pint fresh blueberries
1 pint fresh raspberries
1/2 cup granulated sugar
(garnish) 1 scoops vanilla ice-cream

Method:
1. Preheat oven 375°F.
2. Place pastry squares on a sprayed baking sheet.
3. In a small mixing bowl, combine berries and sugar. Mix well.
4. Place equal amounts of berry mixture in center of each pastry square.
5. Bake for about 30-35 minutes until pastry is golden brown.
6. Serve with ice-cream.

PEANUT BUTTER SMORES

Serving size- 1 party platter, 8 pieces

Ingredients:
1/4 cup butter
8 slices thick white Texas bread
1/2 cup chunky peanut butter
1/2 cup marshmallow fluff
4 large eggs
1 cup 1/2 & 1/2
1 cup graham cracker crumbs
2 tablespoons powdered sugar
(garnish) best ever hot fudge

Method:
1. Melt butter in a large skillet over medium heat.
2. Spread peanut butter and marshmallow fluff evenly over four slices of Texas bread. Top with other four slices of bread to form a sandwich.
3. In a medium mixing bowl, beat eggs and 1/2 & 1/2. Mix well.
4. Dip sandwiches in egg mixture and coat in graham cracker crumbs.
5. Place coated sandwich in skillet and cook for about 5 minutes, flip over and cook another 5 minutes until golden brown.
6. Remove from heat and let cool for 3-4 minutes.
7. Cut sandwiches in half diagonally. Place on a platter and sprinkle with powdered sugar and serve with best ever hot fudge.

CARROT CAKE CUP CAKES
(with a white chocolate cream cheese frosting)

Serving size- 1 party platter, 3 dozen cupcakes

Ingredients:
1 cups vegetable oil
2 cups granulated sugar
5 large eggs
2 3/4 cups all purpose flour
2 teaspoons baking powder
2 teaspoons baking soda
3 teaspoons ground cinnamon
1 teaspoon salt
2 teaspoons maple syrup
2 cups shredded carrots
1 1/2 cups chopped walnuts
1 cup crushed pineapple (drained)
cooking spray

Method:
1. Preheat oven 350°F.
2. In a large mixing bowl, beat oil and sugar together. Add eggs one at a time.
3. Sift together flour, baking powder, baking soda, cinnamon and salt. Add to egg mixture, beating slowly.
4. Add syrup, carrots, walnuts and pineapple. Mix well.
5. Spray muffin pans with cooking spray.
6. Fill muffin tins with carrot mixture 3/4 of the way.
7. Bake muffins for about 35-40 minutes or until inserted toothpick comes out clean. Remove from oven and cool for about 45 minutes.

Frosting:
Ingredients:
1 cup white chocolate chips
1 lb cream cheese (softened)
1 tablespoon vanilla extract
3/4 cup powdered sugar

Method:
1. Place white chocolate chips in a microwave safe bowl and place in microwave oven for 30 seconds. Remove and stir. Place back in the microwave and cook another 30 seconds or until smooth and creamy.
2. In a large mixing bowl, beat cream cheese, vanilla and sugar until smooth and creamy. Add melted white chocolate. Mix well.
3. Refrigerate frosting for about 15 minutes. Ready to frost.

GRANDMA RAY'S APPLE CAKE

Serving size- 1 Bundt cake

Ingredients:
6 granny smith apples (peeled and sliced)
3 tablespoons granulated sugar
2 tablespoons ground cinnamon
1 cup vegetable oil
2 cups granulated sugar
3 cups all-purpose flour
2 tablespoons baking powder
4 large eggs
1/4 cup & 2 tablespoons apple juice
2 1/2 teaspoons vanilla extract
cooking spray
(garnish) powdered sugar

Method:
1. Preheat oven 350°F.
2. In a large mixing bowl, combine sliced apples, 3 tablespoons granulated sugar and cinnamon. Mix well.
3. In another large mixing bowl, combine all other ingredients, one at a time. Mix well.
4. Spray bundt pan with cooking spray.
5. Starting with the batter, layer batter, then apples, then batter, then apples.
6. Bake bundt cake for about 1 hour 15 minutes. Remove from oven and let cool for about 1 hour.
7. Remove bundt cake from pan onto serving plate and sprinkle with powdered sugar.
8. Serve.

Index

Afternoon Fruit Salad, 147
Apple Cinnamon Wontons, 170
Apple Coleslaw, 31
Apple Crusted Pork Chops, 143
Asian Cabbage Pot Stickers, 58
Asian Grilled Tuna Sticks, 113
Baked Halibut Parmesan, 110
Baked Macaroni & Five Cheese Casserole, 70
Baked Potato Salad, 23
Baked Stuffed Chicken Marsala, 128
Baked Stuffed Chicken Parmesan, 131
Baked Stuffed Mushrooms, 57
Baked Stuffed Shrimp, 119
Barry's Favorite Blue Cheese Dressing, 25
Basic Pizza Dough, 102
Beer Battered Asparagus Spears, 86
Beet, Chive & Goat Cheese Tart, 65
Best Ever Hot Fudge, 161
Black Bean Salsa, 16
Blueberry Brown Sugar Pancakes, 157
Blueberry Crumble, 165
Blue Cheese Potato Salad, 21
Breakfast Quesadilla, 150
Broccoli, Kalamata Olive & Feta Cheese Bake, 76
Bruschetta Soup, 2
Buffalo Turkey Wrap, 98
Buttered Leek & Yukon Mash, 82
Cajun Potato Salad, 27
Calamari Fra Diavlo Salad, 34
Calcannon, 78

Caramelized Onion Meat Loaf, 139
Caribbean Red Snapper Filet, 114
Carrot Cake Cupcakes, 175
Cherry Tomato & Mozzarella Kebobs, 38
Chicken Brushetta, 122
Chicken Lemoncello, 127
Chicken Wellington, 130
Chilled Broccolflower Salad, 26
Chilled Grilled Zucchini Salad, 40
Chilled Potato and Green Bean Salad, 41
Chilled Spanish Rice Salad, 20
Chilled Strawberry Champagne Soup, 4
Chili Pepper Crab Dip, 55
Chipotle BBQ Baked Beans, 84
Chipotle Chicken Meltdown, 123
Chipotle Chicken Salad Frisbee's, 37
Chocolate Chip Oatmeal Drop Cookies, 166
Chocolate Snowballs, 167
Chunky Fresh Vegetable Salsa, 10
Classy Chicken Cordon Bleu, 125
Coffee Crusted Sirloin Steaks, 135
Crab and Leek Rangoon's, 60
Creamy Cheddar Chicken Nachos, 53
Creamy Chicken Gorgonzola, 121
Creamy Tomato Gorgonzola, 6
Creole Omelet, 152
Crispy Mushroom Wontons, 63
Curry Salsa, 15
Dijon Crusted Pork Chops, 142
Double Bite Mote Cristo, 158
Double Chocolate Woopie Pies, 164
Drunken Onions, 92
Easy Pulled Pork Quesadilla's, 48
Eggnog French Toast, 151
Englishman's Fried Haddock, 112
Fire Cracker Pizza Sticks, 61

Fire Pit Chili, 3
Forty-Eight Hour Sirloin Tips, 136
Fried Zucchini Spears, 52
Funny Bone Salad, 32
Garden Veggie Slaw, 28
Garlic Crusted Sirloin Steaks, 141
Gaspacho, 7
Gourmet Mushroom, Spinach & Goat Cheese Turnovers, 62
Gramma Ray's Apple Cake, 175
Greek Salad with Fried Eggplant Croutons, 39
Grilled Herbed Marinated Lamb Chops, 144
Grilled Roast Beef Sandwiches, 96
Grilled Turkey Tips, 133
Guinness Battered Chicken Fingers, 45
Herbed Polenta Baked Salmon, 117
Homemade Whipped Cream, 160
Honey Fried Chicken Drumsticks, 124
Irish Potato Croquets, 88
Italian Baked Beans, 73
Italian Muffaletta, 95
Italian Tomato Salsa, 14
Jamaican Jerk Roasted Potatoes, 90
Lamb Bolognese, 145
Lobster Corn Chowda, 8
Lobster & Spinach Calzone, 107
Lemon, Lime & Garlic Grilled Shrimp Sate, 115
Margarita Salad, 22
Marinated Mushrooms, 80
Marshmallow Parfait, 163
Mashed Cauliflower Casserole, 77
Mediterranean Pesto Dip with Pita Bread Chips, 66
Mediterranean Tortellini Salad, 19
Mini Lamb & Goat Cheese Burgers, 99
Mushroom Pomadoro Pizza, 104
Mushroom Stroganoff, 75
Old Fashioned Fried Vidalia Onion Rings, 54

Old Fashioned Home Fries, 153
Orange Curry Chicken Wings, 46
Orzo Confetti Pasta Salad, 36
Oscar Benedict, 154
Pan Fried Spaghetti Martini, 71
Pasta Cobb Salad, 33
Peanut Butter Smores, 172
Peel & Eat Shrimp Martini, 56
Pesto & Crumbled Blue Cheese Stuffed Tomatoes, 91
Pineapple-Coconut-line & Chili Pepper Chicken Sate, 67
Pineapple Salsa, 17
Pistachio Crusted Chicken, 126
Pizza Florentine, 105
Pizza Puttenesca, 103
Poached Salmon Stuffed Jumbo Pasta Shells, 118
Porcupine Potato Croquets, 44
Potato 7 Sour Cream Money Bags, 43
Potato Chip Casserole, 81
Pretzel Crusted Crab Cakes, 49
Pretzel Crusted Mashed Potato Pancakes, 87
Purple Mash Potatoes with Goat Cheese, 74
Quick Baked Stuffed Lobster, 116
Raspberry Baked Brie in Pastry, 64
Red, White & Blue Three Bean Salad, 30
Roast Beef Wrapped Asparagus Spears, 51
Rocky Road Cheesecake, 168
Saucey Meatballs, 59
Sautéed Broccoli Rabe, 72
Savory Herb Bread Pudding Loaf, 85
Seared Filet Mignon, 137
Skillet Mussels, 109
Sloppy B's, 94
Smoked Salmon Cream Cheese Spread, 148
Smoked Salmon Pinwheels, 156
Smoked Salmon Wrapped Sea Scallops, 47
Spicy Baked Beef Taquitos, 50

Spicy Red Pepper Slaw, 29
Spicy Jalapeño Corn Cakes, 89
Spicy Pineapple Braised Beef Short Ribs, 140
Spicy Sausage Calzone, 106
Spicy Scrambled Eggs, 149
Spicy Chopped Sirloin Steaks, 138
Sugar Cane Skewered Sea Scallops, 68
Sugar Coated Fried Flour Tortillas, 169
Surf & Turf Burger, 100
Sweet Potato Salad, 24
Tavern Swordfish, 111
Three Berry Pastry Pillows, 171
Toasted Turkey Cordon Bleu Sandwiches, 97
Tortellini Carbonara, 79
Tortellini Soup, 5
Tuna Salad Lettuce Wraps, 35
Veal Parmesan Burger, 101
Vodka Penne, 83
Warm Creamy Sweet Corn Salsa, 11
White Chocolate Fondue, 162
White Gaspacho Salsa, 13

To Order Copies of

Tasteful Entertaining

by **Chef Barry Keefe**

$19.99

$2.00 Shipping/handling

I.S.B.N. 1-59879-084-6

Order Online at:
www.authorstobelievein.com

By Phone Toll Free at:
1-877-843-1007

By Mail:
Lifevest Publishing
Tasteful Entertaining
4901 E. Dry Creek Road #170
Centennial, Colorado 80122